Screw The

For Driven Women Who Are Ready to Quit Letting Their Bullshit Be Bigger Than Their Dreams

International Amazon Best-Selling Author Katrina Ruth

Published by: Katrina Ruth
Edited by: Deanna Shanti – Shanti Publishing

www.thekatrinaruthshow.com

ISBN: 978-1-950212-00-2

Each month I like to give away courses or books!
Receive this month's FREE in-depth training at:

https://thekatrinaruthshow.com/freegift

For more kickass books including free downloads:
www.booksforkickasswomen.com

Table Of Contents

INTRODUCTION

There is a world out there, which is completely different from anything that the normal person would possibly imagine exists, or even dream about.

It's a world where money is unlimited, where success is completely on your terms, where purpose, passion, alignment, and flow govern everything, and where whatever your heart desires and you set your mind to?

Becomes reality.

It's a world where it's a given that every person you encounter is doing something amazing, something extraordinary, something truly fascinating, and where not only are they 'killing it' in business, but they're also more likely than not to be in a state of fantastic health and fitness, and living with absolute joy and CHOICE, according to their own personal values, in every area of their life.

Business.

Money.

Fitness.

Relationships.

Lifestyle.

ALL of it.

It's the world of having it all, the life you dream of, having it exactly AS you dream of, and have always known you SHOULD, of endless travel and freedom and choice, of fun and laughter and crazy wild adventures, of breaking all the rules and saying a big fuck you to the norm, of doing what you FEEL like doing, not just because you can, but also because you know that when you do?

Everything you ever dreamed of and KNEW you were born for opens up before you, FAST.

This is my world.

This is the world of my friends.

This is the world of my clients.

This is the world of countless people all around the world who dream big -

And are willing to make shit happen.

It's where entrepreneurs, leaders, creators, visionaries and REVOFUCKINGLUTIONARIES come to play life.

And if you're here, and you're reading this, and something inside of you is awakening and saying YES - I fucking KNEW it - then there's really only one more thing I need to say, before we begin:

This is your world too.

Welcome!

We've been waiting for you.

CHAPTER ONE - RESISTANCE

Don't you just find that the real work, the work you were born for, is the work you MOST seem to run from?

I know gorgeous.

OH, how I know. And I am SO here to kick your BUTT on this ... which I love to do, in fact I'm practically levitating in my chair right now, and positively BRIMMING with excitement about it ... but first, I gotta be honest:

I'm as guilty as anyone. Maybe more, since I damn straight should know better!

Truth?

I've resisted writing this book for so long.

The tens of thousands of people who follow me online (thank you!) would possibly disagree with my diagnosis of myself as one who does NOT take action. They see me write every day, share my message and my art, day in and day out, no exceptions, for YEARS now.

One example is that 365 days a year (okay, fine, if we're accurate it's probably 362 days a year!) I write and publish a 1500-2000-word long blog post on Facebook, in various places around the internet.

This is just one way that I "message", and share my art.

I always believed and KNEW I had a message, and something to share with the world. Didn't you?

Yes.

I believe you did!

I also livestream on Facebook nearly every day, post various little missives and rants and ideas, send about 8 emails a day to my online community, document a good portion of what I'm up to and where I'm at in the world on Snapchat, Instagram, Facebook stories (are there stories everywhere now, seriously?!) ... basically, I share a good chunk of my life online.

I don't do this because I think it's what you need to do online ... even though sure; it's made me millions of dollars and much of what I'm going to share in this book will inspire you with the mindset AND the 'how' of that.

But no, it's not something I do for the money or the business success or even the recognition and validation of my writing.

I do it because I can't not.

All I ever wanted to do, really, was to write, speak, motivate, educate and EMPOWER other driven leaders and creators to know:

YES.

What you feel inside of you is real.

YES.

You were born for more.

YES.

That thing you've always had inside of you, of feeling like you have a message, you have a purpose, you were mother-fucking CALLED and you.have.a.DESTINY, one in which you will MAKE millions, IMPACT millions, and change the WORLD ...!

It's all within reach baby.

And it's time to press play.

It's a great story, a true one, too! But here's the missing piece, about me and my REAL art, and perhaps also about you and yours:

The truth is I HAVE been resisting the 'real' work, which is to say the writing of the DEEP soul messages, from me to you, and in this particular FORMAT; a book.

Sure.

I've written books before.

A LOT in fact! I've self-published over 50 books on Amazon ... but there has always been an element of 'one day I'll do the REAL thing'. Whatever that is.

I've decided - this is it baby. I'm doing it. I have NO fucking clue what 'it' even is, but this is me, here, doing it. Showing up. For you. For me. Now!

How it WORKS ... life! ... is that you follow what you feel inside of you.

You don't KNOW the path ahead; that's the point!

But, you know you must take action.

So here I am, doing just that, and TRUSTING that what needs to come out for you, will.

And if what I'm rambling on about resonates with you, there's a very real reason for that:

It's because you too were born for the world of more.

But let's be clear -

As far as this 'make millions of dollars online and just be you' thing (oh yeah! that!) -

For me it happened when I gave in to being who I am, nothing more, and in all its madness.

So as much as I wanna share the 'how' with you, and I will, you have to understand:

The make millions of dollars strategy, or impact millions of people, or plain and simple just know you are doing what you're meant to DO in the world, and that FINALLY that ache inside of you is starting to subside, the hole that was waiting for PURPOSE, is really just this:

Screw the rules.

Just do you.

Which brings me to a question, before we can continue:

Is that you?

Have you always dreamed of more?

Do you KNOW you were freaking born for it?

Are you so damn ready to tap in to how YOU are going to create your empire and COMPLETELY aligned life?

It's time baby.

Enough is enough.

You KNOW you came here to shine!

And there is zero fucking doubt about the fact that you ARE gonna bring it.

Shall we?

CHAPTER TWO – A SINGLE IDEA CAN CHANGE YOUR LIFE

I haven't met Tim Ferriss, yet, but it would be unfair to not mention him right from the get-go here.

Have you read his book, 'The 4-Hour Workweek'? It was released in 2007 and it changed my LIFE. I've read a ton of amazing books. But there are less than 5 I would say truly changed my life. Each of the books which does fit that category I've read over and over again, and Tim's book is most definitely one of them.

The first time I read it, it was one of those moments in time - as I hope it will be for you in reading THIS book, in some way! - when I had something inside of me which I'd ALWAYS known but I suppose never felt sure of, especially of the 'how', completely validated.

Tim spoke about living location free, about getting very, very specific and clear around what your dream life would look like, about calculating exactly how much it would COST to live said dream life, about creating a muse, as he called it, to allow you to do so, and then about going all in to bring that life TO life.

A life in which money and freedom and purpose were on tap, and in which you could do what you want -

When you want -

And with who you want.

NO MATTER HOW BIG OR CRAZY YOU DREAMED.

I'm guessing you probably dream pretty freaking big or crazy, if you've happened into my world, and reading this!

Me too :)

I read the book cover to cover in a day or so, downloaded all of the extra exercises, DID them. I drank the Kool-Aid, every last drop of it, and actively went looking for more. It wasn't something where I thought 'oh, how amazing that would be, imagine!'

It was something where I just very practically and pragmatically thought, yes -

That makes sense.

I'm going to do it.

So let's get started!

And I did.

It was much the same as what I remember feeling when I first picked up my Dad's original copies of various Tony Robbins, Zig Ziglar, Brian Tracy books. I call these authors 'The Godfathers of Personal Development'; even though quite probably the actual OG of personal development was God himself :)

I started reading PD books at the age of 11 or so, picked up off my father's bookshelf, drawn to them as I had such a voracious appetite for reading that I would regularly run out of books from the library to read before I could get back there.

I would read things I didn't understand, and I remember thinking:

Yes.

That's what I'll do.

I'm going to be rich and I'm going to be famous, and I'll be an author and a speaker and make millions and impact millions and change the WORLD!!

You too? In some form? Even without being able to put it into words?

Yes ...

I thought so! Obviously.

And the thing is ... the thing you have to understand and really connect INTO is, that not only is ALL of this (and then some!) possible for you, but that it's your mother-freaking RESPONSIBILITY, baby.

To do the work you were born for.

To FOLLOW the calling inside.

To PRESS fucking play and BE the you who you dream of being such that in doing so you can live the life YOU desire, and also impact others, to do the same.

But here is what you need to understand, if you're resonating, and you're nodding, and you KNOW that you belong here too -

Just because you have a destiny? Doesn't mean you're gonna EVER create it.

Let's talk about that.

CHAPTER THREE – DON'T LET YOUR BULLSHIT BE BIGGER THAN YOUR DREAMS

So last week I paid off a tax bill of $68,654.55. Actually, it was a tax bill of $98,654.55, but I paid the other 30k off over the past 3 weeks already.

Boom.

Boom.

Boom.

And then BOOM motherfucker, take that!

And just like that, for the first time in over 10 years, the time I've been building my business online and creating, along the way, multiple millions of dollars in annual income, I am tax debt free.

Do you ever feel as though something inside of you has this need to HOLD ON to limit, scarcity, lack? The truth is I could DEFINITELY have paid off my tax debts years ago and stayed on top of them. I've been making the MONEY to pay my taxes since day one, because the truth is that even if you're only making a few thousand a year whatever the tax part owed is you CAN afford it. It's a choice.

Manage your freaking money.

Make your payments.

Etcetera.

Even if you don't agree that you CAN afford it on a super low income, I've been out of being TECHNICALLY broke for YEARS now, and I have the lifestyle to prove it! But yet for some reason I still found myself needing to be in scarcity and lack around money.

Making millions.

Feeling broke.

Earlier on, before I was MAKING such money I would have SWORN black and blue that once I start making 'x' amount of

COURSE I'll be on top of things! But the truth is that having more money simply highlights and exacerbates the existing problems you have.

If you think this book is simply a story of inspiration around finding your true soul purpose in life and monetising the fuck out of it, well -

It is!

But part of that story? I'm going to show you how to get REALLY freaking honest with yourself around why you sabotage and hold yourself back, why you seem to have these recurring patterns that just pop up, how it is you can't seem to just FLOW.

Please know:

The flow is waiting for you.

It's ALWAYS been there.

You CAN absolutely make money and a HELLUVA'n impact doing what you love, and on your terms, and you can receive with EASE, and it can all just BE.

But in order to get there you MUST first look at the monsters lurking under the bed.

What are you really scared of?

What are you hiding from?

What are the deep dark fears about what you think might REALLY be in store for you, about how you'll never make it, never be okay, maybe you're not worth it, maybe you shouldn't even EXIST!

I know.

It's horrible to look at.

We're going to do it anyway, but don't worry - it won't hurt too much, not really, and actually? Any small pain you do feel will be WELL fucking worth it, since it will absolutely -

Free you.

And one of the most important things to know of course, is that the money thing, as with most never achieved outcomes, it's never really a conversation about what you're DOING wrong, is it?

It was never that I wasn't good at MANAGING money, although that's what I told myself as I found myself over 100k in debt ... struggling to even buy food at times ... selling my house, my car, my measly share portfolio, even my handbags on eBay, constantly wondering when the FUCK I was going to break through and WHAT was I doing wrong?!

It's not ABOUT why you can't manage your money.

It's your MINDSET that has to be managed, and that motherfucker is a total bitch!!

Your mindset will tell you:

You're not good enough.

You're not worthy.

You SHOULD be living with this shroud and cloud hanging over you.

You DESERVE to struggle, and this is how it's always going to BE.

Never quite there.

Close enough to taste it smell it and KNOW it's waiting.

Yet always -

Falling short.

Do you want to know what it was that changed things for me? Why THIS has become the year, for the first year since I started my online biz, when I've become tax debt free?

Plain and simple baby:

At the start of the year I decided it would be.

Same as how I've achieved EVERY other fucking thing along the way. At some point I got sick of the trying and the planning and even the do, and I just decided:

Fuck this shit.

It's done.

Can I ask you a question? Have you actually DECIDED to ALLOW what it is you long for?

Or are you still letting your bullshit be bigger than your dreams? And if the latter, when do you think you might be done with that, hmmm? I mean ... I know it's COMFORTABLE. But it gets kind of old and tired after a while, RIGHT?!

Of course it could be, that you have a story.

About why it has to be this way.

About how it is. For you, and perhaps even for the whole world as well. About how nobody underSTANDS and everything is conspiring AGAINST you and you really, really ARE trying to get ahead!

And I'll say to you:

I know a thing or two about stories. So let me tell you some, but let's start with a story of ACTUALLY saying 'fuck this shit', in a real way, to EVERY single freaking tie that binds you.

Lean in ...

Listen closely ...

This is where the eyes wide open slap on the face WAKE-the-fuck-up call happens. Or, you know - where you see your own bullshit, maybe for the first time ever, and decide that FINALLY you're going to allow your dreams, your desires, your truth, your yes, to receive more of you.

CHAPTER FOUR – FUCK THIS SHIT

I have nothing to say.

CHAPTER FIVE – SOMEHOW YOU JUST KEEP GOING. THAT'S HOW IT'S DONE.

I just DESTROYED my legs in Seminyak, Bali's 'The Daily Gym', and practically fell over walking back to my villa. Now, I sit here, a glass of oddly PURE tasting cold drip coffee by my side, a single large ice-drop immersed in it, ready to write, to you.

Yesterday I thought that resistance had me beat, but actually it lost. Ha! Take THAT, fucker! What I find is, what YOU will find is, and maybe already do, that the more you just show up and make SPACE for your art, the faster and further into flow you're able to drop.

This is not exactly an unknown concept to me ... it's only the exact way I've built my entire online empire these past 11+ years! But yes, when it comes to writing THIS book, resistance has, as I've mentioned, been a bitch. However, my rule is simple, and it's one I'd love to share with you as you can use it to achieve EXTRAORDINARY and life-changing results in ANYTHING:

Show up.

Daily.

Do the work.

Daily.

Whether you feel like it or whether you don't, and also regardless of whether or not you think it's any GOOD!

Repeat.

(Daily)

I KNOW.

UGH!

Even right now as I sit here, I'm just thinking about how UNCOMFORTABLE it feels to me to be working on a book; one which I know is TRUE purpose work. It's easy for me to do what I do in my online world each day! But to chase after a deeper soul work goal? Ugh! So.Fucking.Hard.

But, there you have it! It is what it is.

In fact, I'm pretty sure that the more you want to RUN from a thing, the more important it is ...

So, now that this book has begun itself, there is zero doubt that it will be finished.

I've self-published 50+ small books on Amazon already using the *'just show up and write'* technique.

And I've also built an online success mentoring business which makes millions each year by doing the same.

My most magical success strategy is simply to be fucking consistent! DISCIPLINE, baby, and motherfucking habit. NO MATTER WHAT.

My agreement with myself, thus far, for this book, is 1000 words per day. Minimum. If the flow takes over, well - shit might just get a little bit faster | crazier | more fun still! Don't you just LOVE how once you get started with your purpose work you ALWAYS find it's actually so much easier than what you thought?!

I wonder what YOU could get into flow with, so much easier than what you think, if you just committed to that first stage?!

It's certainly something to think about ...

We'll come back to that later. For now, let's get back to this:

CHAPTER SIX – FUCK THIS SHIT (FOR REAL NOW)

I believe that every single artist | creator | revolutionary | leader who has actually created even a single THING of note, and in particular those VERY rare few who actually unleash their purpose work, the PAINFUL raw work of their soul, has at some point reached what can REALLY only be termed a 'fuck this shit' moment.

You may have experienced this already, perhaps, maybe even for your soul work?

Perhaps you, like me, can hand on your heart say YES. I'm doing it. I'm finally fucking DOING it! Of course, if you CAN, then you'll also know what all true artists know, which is that - God damn it! - the layers are never fully peeled back, are they?

Just when you think you already went all in ...

And that (look at ME!) you're doing it ...

You realise:

Oh fuck.

I've barely even begun.

The TRUE way to know you're an artist is if every day you wake up and realise that once again, you have to go back into the SAME FUCKING BATTLE AND FRAY, just deeper. It'd be a total BITCH really (and kinda is anyway) if it weren't for that fact that the horror of NOT being this kind of person means that you practically want to kiss the floor in gratitude that you ARE, whenever you actually stop and think about it.

Side note:

STOP AND FUCKING THINK ABOUT IT AND THEN GO KISS THE FLOOR!

IMAGINE if you weren't this kind of person!!

Really!!

Actually, before I get more into the fucking of the shit (lol), I'd love to share with you a blog which I wrote today, that I think might just speak to your soul.

I publish a blog - I call it The Daily Asskickery - nearly every single day, 360+ a year. If you'd like to receive some of these blogs from me on email - you can go to www.katloterzo.com/freegift and register. Be warned that you'll also officially become part of my online tribe of crazy mad AF creators who are doing the work to live the life they desire! Shit gets pretty crazy in there!

Not only will you get ME kicking your butt into alignment and massive fucking action in your inbox each day (eek!) you'll also get a free gift. Can't tell you what it is though, except that it's something I USED to sell for real actual money!!

So here is today's Daily Asskickery blog:

SO YOU DON'T FEEL LIKE IT, YOU'RE SCARED AND TIRED DAY AFTER DAY, AND FRANKLY YOU WISH THE WHOLE WORLD WOULD FUCK THE FUCK OFF? CONGRATULATIONS ... YOU'RE AN ARTIST.

I don't know if you know this, but the whole entire world does NOT wake up every day with dread and fear and resistance hanging over them as they wonder, yet again, if they'll have what it takes today to show up and do the WORK, of living life purposefully.

I know it seems ridiculous ... mind-blowing ... even (to me!) IMPOSSIBLE to believe, but I have it on good authority that the majority of people out there actually accept and are content with their lives.

The worst part? This is true even for most so-called entrepreneurs and creators.

Me, I find it hard to distinguish, really, between entrepreneur and artist. I can't relate to the idea of being JUST about biz and money, because for me it's always been about the art, the purpose, the NEVER-ending burning need to release, and the truth is I do think that anybody who is TRULY an entrepreneur who 'can't not', is also, in their own way, however that might be, an artist.

To monetize IS to create.

And if you're smart about it (which we ARE!) - then to create is to monetize. With EASE baby!

And here is how you know for sure that YOU are for real, that you belong in this crazy world of DRIVEN creators; the ones who will ultimately rule and also CHANGE the world; wake it up -

You know because every single day feels like a battle to the death.

I know, I know, what a thing to say! For somebody who talks all of the time about flow. About going WITH said flow. About simply tuning in and following the call, letting it be easy, letting it be effortless, doing only what you are CALLED to do.

The funny thing is - and I think that very few, well, only the RIGHT few, will ever understand this - you can be in flow and in ease and in absolute alignment and you can also want to scream “fuck the WORLD” and run and hide and not FEEL like it.

Sometimes???

MUCH of the time!

I believe that if you're not regularly waging war against the demon within who tells you to take today off, to rest easy, or to simply do the work that actually FEELS easy, and to put off the GROWTH stuff, or the REAL stuff, then you're not actually on PURPOSE and you're not actually an artist.

You may call yourself one.

And you may even be CREATING.

In fact, you might have fallen prey to one of the most deceptive realities of all: to be successful in business or as an artist, so much so that you have convinced the whole world and even yourself that you DID it, you BEAT resistance, you showed up and LOOK HOW FREAKING AWESOME YOU ARE ...

But that deep down.

Every damn day.

In every damn way.

You're living with the knowledge that you're avoiding your ACTUAL work.

And there's no way to argue against that, is there? It just IS. You KNOW if you're not doing THE.ACTUAL.WORK, and no matter how 'close to' the actual work what you are doing instead is, the work is the work and there is no way to replace the energy of what you WOULD be feeling right now if you were doing THE work.

But if you think that doing THE work is something that you just dance and spring your way into, merrily, day after day, then think the fuck again, because that's not how it IS.

Look through the journals and pages of any artist who showed up and unleashed their ACTUAL truth, and you will see that it's messy, painful, scary, EXCRUCIATING even, and that the mind will do EVERY POSSIBLE THING to talk you out of it, and that's all before BREAKFAST.

So let me tell you.

What it feels like.

To be an artist.

Who looks the beast in the eye and then does the TRUE work, anyway.

You wake up, and already the feeling is hanging over you. Will I today? Can I? Will I actually UNLEASH?

Your mind starts to play games right away, about all that there is to do instead, convincing you that doing SOME work is the work, trying to trick you away from facing in to your actual soul and truth.

You start to make a story. Which could be that today you just need to REST ... today is a day of self-care, yes, that's it! Or else you listen to the story that if you follow the trick, and you busy yourself, with perhaps even GOOD and CREATIVE and FLOW based work, just not THE actual work, that that will be good enough, for today, and that maybe even that's what you SHOULD do, today.

Perhaps you listen to the story and your day passes accordingly ...

Or perhaps not.

It doesn't get easier once out of bed. There are SO many things to take you away from your art.

Maybe you need to eat, or perhaps you just need to check in, maybe you really ARE tired or burnt out and you should go get a MASSAGE or meditate, yes that's it!

You tell yourself 1000 stories.

Before the sun has barely even risen.

And if you're like 99.99% of people, yes even so-called creatives, then obviously, you listen, and your whole life, is created, accordingly.

By NOT doing what you came here to do.

If you're (truly) one of us ... an artist who also DOES their art ... which is an extraordinary thing indeed ... then you manage, step by step and breath by breath, to not LISTEN to the stories.

You grit your teeth.

You turn away.

You turn WITHIN.

And you ask yourself, even though you REALLY wish you didn't have to, what do I actually NEED right now?

And piece by piece, breath by breath, moment by moment you manage to NOT LET RESISTANCE RULE YOU.

What you have to understand, is that if you think there's going to be some magical time when you just ALWAYS WANT TO BARE YOUR NAKED SOUL AND LET OUT THE ART FROM YOUR CORE then your idea of what ART is, is based on surface bullshit that is not the TRUTH.

To be an artist is to turn your insides out every damn day, whether you feel like it or whether you don't.

OF COURSE IT FUCKING HURTS!!

And what the WANNABE artists will never understand is that the BEAUTY, the FLOW, the YES, the ORGASMIC ENERGY of doing what you were BORN for can truly only come FROM being the rare one who faces INTO that pain, that fear, that "I CAN'T today" feeling every damn DAY, and then does it anyway.

I can't tell you how often I have to CONSCIOUSLY turn away from what my mind TRICKS me into thinking I need, in order to do my SOUL work.

It might be the obvious tricks, such as telling me I'm not tired today, I don't feel like it today, I have nothing to SAY today, anyway, and besides - I already DID enough.

That's easy.

I know those tricks from since before time began.

I'm sure you do too.

Don't feel like it, don't know how, scared, tired, whatever.

Too bad!

Show up.

Do the work.

But it's so much more than that, isn't it?

It's feeling hunger and saying no, I haven't done the work yet.

It's having a million things that want your attention, and are also valid, and saying no, I haven't done the work yet.

It's seeing that if you don't get on with your gym or your errands or your what-ever, then you'll run out of time, and saying no, I haven't done the WORK yet.

It's feeling that maybe you truly DO need to take pause, re-set, maybe you're PUSHING OUTSIDE OF FLOW, and realising that THIS lie is the most insidious of all and saying NO bitch, I haven't done the God.Damn.Work yet!

It's beginning, actually beginning, and putting that time aside, and stepping forth and then not FEELING anything, not connecting to anything, and starting to wonder if you should just come back to it later when inspiration or flow strikes and saying NO, I haven't done the WORK yet and I will damn well SIT my ass here in this chair until it's done!

It's being committed, above all else, to the routine or process which you can DEPEND UPON to lead you INTO the work, and then doing it.

When the rest of the world.

Is doing whatever the fuck it is they do.

Or even your own conniving mind is telling you.

That today is a day to stop.

And instead you turn away -

Once again.

And you turn within -

Once more.

And you do the THINGS.

You follow your process and then when it's time you BEGIN. Knowing that the flow will come to YOU, that the muse visits only those who CONSISTENTLY put themselves in a position of being PRESENT AND IN ATTENDANCE to be so blessed.

And sure enough.

Every day.

You get the job done and you step INTO flow.

But no.

You don't sit back.

And wait for it.

That's not how it WORKS.

So, if you find yourself day after day feeling scared, unsure, not knowing how you can possibly get through and terrified that today will be the day you have your deepest fears - of not actually having anything real inside of you - proven?

And then you show up anyway and you do the ACTUAL FUCKING WORK THAT EATS AT YOUR SOUL?

Congratulations baby.

You're an artist, a messenger, a creator, born for more!

NOT JUST ONE WHO HAS IT INSIDE OF THEM.

A successful person in the world's eye is somebody who typically has managed to ignore their art every day in order to create results.

An artist is somebody who manages to ignore normal-world success every day in order to do their art.

Make no mistake: YOU CAN HAVE IT ALL.

But don't let success and 'doing the work' continue to stop you from baring your SOUL.

Please.

Do the work you came here to do.

It's the ONLY way to get where you truly long to go.

Remember ...

Life is Now. Press Play.

Kat

PS ... gorgeous are you an artist who is called and also ready to let the REAL work BE the work, get it done, and ALLOW it to grow you a mother-fucking EMPIRE?

I show DRIVEN artist entrepreneurs, the ACTUAL 1% within the 1% how to get the fuck out of their own way, do the REAL work, and also monetize that shit to the tune of multiple-millions of dollars of SOUL aligned income, per year, all online.

Ready to biz, art, money, life, COMPLETELY on your terms?

Rich Hot Empire starts next Monday, and it is THE most successful rapid-result mentoring program online for crazy as fuck creators who want it all, on their terms.

In 6 weeks you'll get more done than most people manage in 2 years online, or at all, and that's a FACT. Just ask anybody who has done the work with me in RHE.

Ready to step up? Know (even if it scares you a little!) that I am the mentor to kick your butt in doing so?

Message me NOW to talk then, and for all the details.

You get me on tap 24/7.

And a FULL 'what to do and how to do it' of exploding an online empire, with your soulmate tribe, and multiple streams of recurring and automated income on flow.

Time to stop talking about making this your life ... and to actually get it done baby.

CHAPTER SEVEN - THIS IS HOW I SELL ONLINE

I nearly took the CTA ("call to action") at the end of the blog I just shared out. Then I realised - how freakin' selfish that would be! What better way to demonstrate to you what it is I do each day to run / grow this empire and UNLEASH my purpose work, than to share a live example.

I'll talk more about it later ... and of course ultimately, it's all about finding your OWN true path not needing to worry about how I do it and what the 'strategy' is (it's screw the rules and do you; we talked about that!) ... but just so you know, that's all I do.

Show up each day.

Unleash what's inside of me to say.

Make a call to action to whatever it is I'm feeling called to offer in that moment and / or have created and unleashed that week.

Repeat.

The offer I made at the end of today's blog, for Rich Hot Empire, applies several times a year for those who are called to work with me at that level, so by all means if it spoke to you - message me on Facebook!

Feel free to message me anytime on Facebook anyway, actually! I'd for real love to hear from you. Aside from writing, speaking, creating, and hanging out inside my OWN crazy mind, what I love more than anything is hanging out with my SOUL TRIBE. That's you baby ... so if I'm inspiring, motivating, educating, empowering YOU to press play, then let me know, and come say hi.

Let's play life together!

CHAPTER EIGHT - BACK TO THE POINT!

Okay, MAN - you'd think I could get to the point EVENTUALLY, wouldn't you?! Of course, if you know me you'll soon realise that if you DO indeed think that you'd be dead WRONG. Just come watch my nearly daily Facebook livestreams if you want a daily example of the message, and the being of 'me', taking me wherever the fuck it damn well pleases.

But YESSSSSS ... I DO want to tell you about the fuck this shit moment I alluded to a few chapters back.

I want to tell you about mine.

And I also want to dig in, fully, to YOURS, and maybe, just maybe let that shit come OUT, so that YOU can finally be done enough with your own BS to let the world see the REAL you.

The fuck this shit moment is--

CHAPTER NINE -FUCK THIS SHIT!!

Side note - there's something magical about Bali, for unleashing the true work. I strongly recommend you find a way to get yourself there!

Okay.

Back to it.

Mind you -

I feel as though the fuck this shit story is kind of told already, don't you?

The point clearly doesn't want to be made any more than it already has been! But just in case you're not sure, here goes:

You live your life out of alignment, off path, NOT being fully true to yourself for so long ... always trying, always seeking, to get into alignment, to slip into flow, to OWN who you are and what you want.

And you make steps, of course! You PRO-GRESS! You achieve! And then one day you wake up, and realise, that the being of a Superwoman or Superman (you) whilst certainly IMPRESSIVE, is not what it's actually meant to BE about.

Yes, you have done Many Very Important Things. You are proud of them! You are proud of YOU!

But, you want more.

So much more.

And you're not being honest.

Completely.

Or maybe at all.

About what MORE would actually look like.

And perhaps something happens, or perhaps nothing at all, and one morning you wake up, or one day the passion of God himself is charged into you and you stand up straight and THROW your hands to the heavens and with passionate certainty you proclaim:

FUCK.

THIS.

SHIT.

It's actually a critical part, you'll find, on the road to screwing the RULES, and just doing you.

For me, it was simple. I had to reach a point of allowing life and my OWN FEAR OR SCARCITY BASED CHOICES to break me so much that I could eventually realise and be HONEST about the fact that I wanted SO.MUCH.MORE.

So, I drew my line in the sand.

Fuck this shit.

I decided.

Fuck this shit.

And I made a decision -

Fuck.

This.

Shit!

And also, to put it into more 'actionable' words -

That from that day forward? I would COMPLETELY own who I am. Write what I want, say what I want, show UP how I want and ON MY TERMS.

Of course, the truth is you must make such a decision a million times in your life, and perhaps more. I've made it many times since. But I can tell you that to TRULY look within and admit what I wanted and who I came here to be?

It awoke something in me.

I would not be writing this book without it.

In fact, my entire online empire wouldn't exist without it.

Because here is the truth:

When you DECIDE TO BE YOU and you then GO ALL IN AND ACTUALLY DO SO?

The world will create itself around you to allow it.

So, say it with me:

Fuck THIS shit.

Screw the rules.

It's time to do me!

CHAPTER TEN - A STORY ABOUT WHAT IT'S LIKE TO COACH A 7-FIGURE CLIENT AND WATCH HER GROW.

Part of me feels a little anxious that I'm not giving you some kind of step-by-step strategy of how to screw the rules and do you. I'm sitting here and the voice inside my head is taunting me right now -

"Who the hell do you actually think you ARE? How is all THIS woo-woo blah blah going to help anybody? Do you really think this can be a BOOK; a real one? IT'S NOT EVEN GOING IN ANY SORT OF PROPER ORDER, and besides - when were you thinking of telling people where to START, what to do next, what after that?!"

I feel all this washing through me, and I worry -

SHOULD I write this in the way that 'normal' books are written? SHOULD I write it so that it speaks TO the normal person? SHOULD I write it in a way that makes sense according to The Powers That Be of the Book World?

Help!

Of course, there's one MAJOR problem with that, even if I wanted to:

I can either screw the rules and be ME -

Or I can churn out some bland as fuck bullshit which my heart and soul is not REMOTELY into, and which is not even my true message or ART, and therefore can't POSSIBLY do what it was meant to do for you, just so I can say 'yay, I wrote a book the way it was meant to be written'.

I mean ... apparently there are RULES. Apparently, there is a right way and a wrong way to DO this damn thing! Wanna know an embarrassing secret??

I tried the right way, late last year. I KNEW I had to write this book, with this title. But, I tried to follow A Very Proper Book Plan.

Before I'd even begun the first outline, it was already dead to me.

I was so bored. And to be honest, I was disheartened. Was this how it had to be; if I wanted to be REALLY known as a writer?

So, I walked away.

Now, I'm back, because the ART WILL COME OUT, and I KNOW that what I have to share with you is real, but yet STILL there is that voice inside my head saying YOU HAVE TO FOLLOW THE RULES OR YOU'RE GONNA FAIL ... MAKE A FOOL OF YOURSELF ... BE A COMPLETE.FUCKING.LOSER.

I KNOW you're familiar with that voice!!

Well, there's only one thing for it:

SCREW that bitch.

FUCK her right in the face.

Okay, that's probably too full on. I bet that's gonna get edited out when I'm not watching, ha! But, fuck it - KEEP IT IN PEOPLE WHO READ THIS.

It's necessary.

And besides, as far as me telling you the 'how' on how to screw the rules and do you; ain't THAT a fine and dandy idea of ridiculousness?!

I think you'll get -

From reading this -

PRECISELY what you need to.

In precisely the WAY you were meant to.

Okay?

Okay!

Where was I?

WRITING, about 7-figure badasses online!

I THINK I had something else I was going to say to you before this, but before I sat down for today's book writing, I was on a Facebook Messenger call with my client Amanda Frances.

Amanda came to me last year when her goal was to have her first $500,000 year.

She achieved that.

She's now on track with her first 7-figure year (right away the year after, of course!)

Actually, this time last week Amanda was right here in Bali with me; she flew out from Santa Barbara to see me, and we spent Friday playing life.

Did I say playing life? I mean a client VIP day, for her business, of course :)

The thing you have to know, if you truly want to peer into this world and perhaps even join us here, is that to play business IS to play life.

I posted the following on Facebook just now, about our call, alongside a pic of me sitting on the Bali street. You can see it here, and come say hi to me on Facebook, if you'd like:

http://bit.ly/2DSTHI0

I'd love you to read the comments on that post, if you want to see how for REAL I am with how this world works. My clients are my friends, are my sisters, are my mentors, and we truly just have WAYYYYYY too much fun. I feel like it has to be seen to be believed and that even then you probably won't believe it.

The thing is ... life is SUPPOSED to be easy and flow based and CRAZY ass fun!! Whoever invented this VERY odd idea of 'work' being a bad thing is just ... I mean ... man. I don't even know! Just - don't talk to that person, okay?!

Here's what I wrote:

"This is the face of a mentor who is so in love with her clients it's just not funny.

As Amanda Frances just said to me at the end of our coaching call, which I ran sitting right here on the street in Bali outside my favourite cafe ... we are SO damn good at life.

My clients are my friends, my #soulsisters and my confidantes as much as I am theirs, and also, honoured and humble to MENTOR them.

Of course, when I coach my clients we talk about their biz, their money, their impact, their GROWTH. We do the work.

But the truth is that once you begin playing at a certain level ... the 7-figure level and beyond, which I'm proud to say I have quite a few private clients playing happily at, with ease ... the conversation just slips ever more into LIFE.

On our call just now, we spoke about:

* Being completely crazy and a hot mess, of COURSE

* Team and growth and OWNING being the CEO of a 7-figure / multi-7-figure biz

* Conscious ALLOWANCE around having a flat stomach and detoxing with ease

* Minimum standards for lifestyle (VIFP, obviously)

* The difference between SPENDING and INVESTING (affirmation: 'everything I spend into my business is returned to me 10x over')

* Tindering with intention (the only way!) and how we like to be treated on a date (starting with EXACTLY how the pick up to start the date should go)

This is business.

This is life.

This is being the 1% of the 1% of entrepreneurs, leaders, artists, owning it, calling it in, and playing in that space.

Welcome to our world ..."

***

Do you see how easy it can be?

Do you FEEL how for real this is?

Do you REALISE that this is all freaking POSSIBLE, for you?!

In case you've not yet figured it out, my mission with this book is to not only awaken your eyes to what is POSSIBLE, but also to invite you to come play life with us.

I think you know

Already

If your soul is calling you

To come join us!!

And to find your path.

Pssst ... you can do that for FREE, here - plus get cool stuff! www.katloterzo.com/freegift

CHAPTER ELEVEN - EYES ON YOUR OWN PATH BABY!

There is so much I want to tell you gorgeous.

So many things, so many IMPORTANT things I have to say, about the truth of this journey, and being one of US.

One who insists on doing things their way.

Who says, 'fuck the rules', thank you very much and I'll figure it OUT.

Who walks away.

From even the IDEA of manufactured fame, or success.

And who knows, deep within her core, that what she feels inside her is real and she CAN have it all.

I'm sitting outdoors now in the Bali night, the pool of my private villa bubbling away ... listening to Airplanes Part II (Eminem & Hayley Williams version) ... drinking Bordeaux from the fancy wine bar at the end of the street ... of course I manage to stay at a place right near the only fancy wine bar on this whole island :) ... and thinking of the conversation I just had with my friend and previous client, Naomi, at dinner.

About the madness of the entrepreneur and creator world, and the fact that at some point so many seem to have forgotten it was all supposed to be about standing up and creating what you believe in, and now it's a mixture of the blind leading the blind or some kind of horrible high school clique situation.

About how critical it is to stay true to yourself when it's so easy to fall prey to the 'rules' of how to stand out or be known.

About how even the TINIEST compromise means you're not in alignment and that actually, there is no need for compromise at all and that to give IN to it, for want of money, fame, success, anything, is to give in to not being YOU.

When I spend time with any of the amazing people I've met through living this life - and I continue to meet new ones nearly every day - I am repeatedly in awe and gratitude over the fact that I get to live like this, have friends like this, do business like this.

Can you imagine living a life where every conversation just flows and flies ... you and the other person walk out elevated just by being in the presence of the other ... you learn more about who you are and what you STAND for simply by breaking bread (or, lychee martini!) together?

Last night I went on a date, a walk on the beach, a few drinks at a bar, a nice enough night, and okay I'll admit it, it was someone I met on Tinder, and honestly all I could think?

Well, this is NICE ... but really. I'd kind of rather be working. I just lost three hours during which I could have been writing! And I energetically pushed him away until he left. Lol.

And then I go to dinner.

With a client.

Who has, of course, become a friend.

Follow it up with a Bali massage, a one hour stop to release pain on my walk home.

And once again.

The world makes sense.

Don't you just think the whole POINT is that you DO get to create the world around you?!

You get to choose:

Who you are.

How you show up.

How you make money.

What it's all about.

Who you surround yourself with.

How to LIVE, every damn PART of it.

But here's the thing, and the 'catch', for those who crave to live like this:

It takes fucking guts, gorgeous.

It takes being freaking HONEST with yourself.

And it takes doing what EVER is necessary in order to create your path the way you dreamed of it.

It takes turning away.

From ANYTHING that is not this.

And turning in.

To the God damn truth.

I want to share with you how I recently made the choice to tune in, and act from truth ... and in actuality, had this not happened? This book you're reading would not exist.

Walking away from what is not right -

Is how you make space for what is.

PLEASE: 100% alignment and yes, or WALK THE FUCK AWAY.

CHAPTER TWELVE - I JUST WALKED AWAY FROM 2 POSSIBLE TELEVISION SHOW OFFERS, AND AN IN-CONVERSATION DEAL WITH TARGET AMERICA ...

Less than a minute ago I sent an email which nearly made me vomit, yet I know COMPLETELY and fully it was the right thing to do.

I was on the verge of signing a contract for, essentially, lifelong 'fame management' with an undisputedly badass team who currently BRING it for their A-list clients across a range of industries.

It was a contract which would require $2.8 million in marketing investment from me, over the next 18 months, although I suppose that's neither here nor there :)

It was a contract which was WAITING to be signed, over the past several weeks, as I went back and forth with my solicitor, fine-tuning points of detail which increasingly made me wonder -

All manner of things. Mostly, that the more you have to worry over detail ... the less things DO tend to be a 'hell yes'.

But I pressed forward, because there were BIG things on the line, and besides, my agent had ASSURED me that I would be able to do 'whatever the fuck I want', artistically.

And that every deal they'd pitched had been ACCEPTED, even with me being the cursing, unpredictable badass I am. America wants a new darling, apparently, and one with sass and edge :)

And the plan was for me to be that person. I know this sounds extreme, but it was for me to REPLACE the likes of Ellen, Oprah, Wendy Williams, in the talk show space.

To be the "I'll Make You Rich and Happy" Millionaire Mentor, with the empire | product range | A-list cred to match.

And you know what? I believed in it. I STILL believe it was all possible. And I believe that it WAS about being true to the art ... that the team I was working with DO believe in my craziness ... that they DO want to let ME be me.

But yet ...

Something inside me, the whole time, has felt -

Just not.

HELL TO THE YES.

In fact, I already backed away a few weeks ago!!

And said -

I can't. It doesn't feel aligned. I feel as though I'm going to become TRAPPED, into conformity, and performance, on command.

I was assured I'd have ABSOLUTE freedom, and they basically 're-sold' me on plan fame, very effectively, and I agreed to go back in.

But the thing is ...

Absolute freedom ...

Is actually not POSSIBLE if you say yes to filming ten days out of every month, on the other side of the world, plus travel time, on a schedule, and with performance needing to be BROUGHT!

What if I don't feel like filming that day?

What if I don't feel like covering the topic that was decided?

WHAT IF IT'S MY OWN CHILD'S BIRTHDAY THAT DAY?

Apparently, I don't want it as much as I said I did :)

But there's a bigger issue at play here:

I always thought -

That when I became famous -

It would be because I broke all the rules, did it my way, invented a NEW way, something that makes people wonder, and proclaim, and stare.

And this ...

Does not feel like that.

This ...

Feels like giving in. To ego. To the manufacturing. Of a celebrity. A star. A VERSION, of me, who even though she is 'allowed to say what she wants' is obviously going to still end up doing it in SOME way on command and for a CHOSEN and marketed to audience.

And I'm all about the #culttribe baby.

Not the chosen and marketed to niche.

To quote Amanda Palmer, whose book 'The Art of Asking' I adore: "WE ARE THE MEDIA!"

And also ...

I realised. As much as I tried not to admit it, or to reframe it.

-

I was in some way stating:

"I might not be able to do this myself. I should sign over a percentage of my income for LIFE and agree to jumping through even the SMALLEST of hoops in order to get to my goals"

TALK ABOUT HYPOCRITICAL!!

And then, and yes this definitely does influence me -

I read stories. A lot of books and stories. Of truly CRAZY creators and artists. And there is a common fucking theme that runs through them.

THE MANAGER THING ALWAYS ENDS IN TEARS.

Because really, how can it NOT, no matter how well-intentioned the manager is, when by DEFINITION their job is to 'help you be a better you'.

Remember:

Screw the rules.

JUST DO YOU.

NOT - "just do you based on the recommended pathway!"

I decided to pay attention, finally, to the stories.

I decided to pay attention, finally, to the fact that I shouldn't NEED to nut out or feel into SO MANY GOD DAMN DETAILS.

I decided to pay attention, finally, to the deep set but DAMN firm belief that I will DO IT MY WAY.

On my terms.

I'll go ALL the way.

But I won't sacrifice ANYTHING to do so, that I'm not doing willingly.

I decided to listen to my fucking gut.

And now I can breathe again :)

I'm flying free baby. It's just me and me to get me to the top.

And it's gonna be the best ride ever :)

Also - Here is the email I sent:

"Over the weekend I was really called to dig deep into this agreement and what it would mean for me; whether it's in keeping with my higher values and purpose. The past week or so I've been feeling increasingly gut-pulled to NOT go ahead.

For reasons, purely, of - intuition. Around venturing down a management pathway at ALL. If I were to do so, it would absolutely be with you; my decision is around deciding NOT to do so, and in line with that to also NOT pursue television / traditional media, at this stage.

And long story short ... after essentially meditating on it the entire flight back to Australia yesterday ... it is not in alignment for me.

I could expand, if you like, but I don't know that it serves a purpose, and it won't change things.

I was so certain, or thought I was, to the tune of obviously going back and forth with my solicitor on our agreement multiple times and also locking in my travel dates for upcoming work; this has only become properly clear to me in the past three or so days, and more so over the past twenty-four hours as I actually stopped mentally avoiding it and dug deep.

I am truly sorry for the inconvenience, and regret it deeply, although I couldn't have made this decision sooner or else, would have.

All the best -

Kat"

PPS Want to know the thing which tipped me over the edge? It was my beautiful niece, Scarlett's, first birthday just a week or so ago. My sister Jess already delayed the party until late May as I was previously booked to be in the US in April. I said yes of COURSE I will be there. And then realised, I had to go to Philadelphia to film that same week. To get the fame game rolling.

But that's the way it goes, right? I couldn't bring myself to tell Jess yet, who didn't so much as miss a step of MY daughters first year of life, but I accepted that such is life. She'd understand...

And then over the weekend, it hit me: that's not how I want to live my life. I will NOT look back on endless years of things that I DO want to be part of, missed.

I fucking love that beautiful baby and I WANT TO BE THERE. And I said I would :) So I'll be damned if I'm gonna renege on it, and actually, no matter how much I talk about fame and fortune, I don't care that much.

Besides: FUCK THE HOW. And I don't care for this particular how!!

I won't give my life for it if it comes before PURPOSE, and PURPOSE means I get to have it ALL.

If I thought that 'it all' meant spending half my month every month for the foreseeable future filming to get famous, I'd damn well do it.

But, I don't.

It was always meant to be about making it up as I go, throwing shit at the internet and indeed now the whole world, but having to follow a SCHEDULE??

Perform on COMMAND?

Even for THAT level of being seen?

No.

To me, teetering on the edge of that decision, about Scarlett's birthday, represented everything.

And besides ... it was always meant to be about me doing me, however the fuck I want.

#THEARTBABY #always #theart #WEARETHEMEDIA

CHAPTER THIRTEEN -BROKEN, PERFECT, STUCK, FUCKED UP, IN FLOW, ALIGNED, NO IDEA HOW OR WHAT OR WHY, BUT ABSOLUTELY SO WHERE YOU NEED TO BE.

When you feel broken and stuck and so fucked up and as though you have nothing to give, nothing to say, you know nothing at all, and are not even sure who you are, just remember:

Eyes on your own path.

One foot forward.

Repeat.

When you find yourself wandering, in circles, in the depths and murk of your own mind, like a cat who refuses to settle for a sleep, stop-starting and second guessing so many times that you're about ready to scream, just remember:

Eyes forward.

On your path.

Take a step.

When all you can hear is the voices inside your head and your starting to wonder if the monster under the bed is maybe REAL, just remember:

Eyes on your own path.

MOVE.

When you don't want to -

When you really just can't EVEN -

When it all seems empty -

And stale -

And you start to believe -

The bullshit -

That it's about waiting for inspiration, that it's valid to not show up until the muse does first, that you must go MORE within and maybe NEVER come out, just REMEMBER:

Eyes up.

Check your path.

Move INTO it.

Would you like to know the difference between an artist, a messenger, a leader, a creator, who never is known, because they never fucking let it out, let alone DID anything with it, and one who MAKES it, steps into their every dream?

The latter showed the fuck up.

For their dreams.

For their life.

Broken, perfect, stuck, aligned, it's ACTUALLY all the same thing anyway.

It's all just a moment in time -

When you stop.

And you DECIDE.

This is who I am, this is what's going on right now, and so it MEANS THIS.

And if I'm THIS ... then it means I have to THAT ... or not ...!

And I think:

Sure, but the only way forward regardless of whether or not ANY of this is true?

Eyes on your own path.

Keep on keeping on.

And I totally believe that right now I'm writing COMPLETE FUCKING BULLSHIT because I feel stuck and stunted and empty in my mind/my heart and maybe even my soul and I have nothing to give and so I am completely just making up RUBBISH in order to fill space and somehow try to shift this really odd energy I'm in since writing a pussy massage blog (#eek!) yesterday -

And then at the same time I also know:

Yes ...

But there will be somebody.

One person.

Maybe more.

But somebody.

Who for some reason I could NEVER possibly fathom, will need to read EXACTLY FUCKING THIS TODAY.

And even if that weren't true (and it always is), what is most CERTAINLY true is that the pro shows up.

Day in.

Day out.

Chasing that motherfucking muse down.

Because it's air to us to do so.

We can't breathe without this work.

We will die for this work.

So we might as well fucking live for it before we do.

CHAPTER FOURTEEN - LET'S TALK ABOUT THE THING. WHICH YOU'VE BEEN IGNORING. AND IT'S TIME, TO DO, NOW.

Can we talk about the thing gorgeous? The thing you've been ignoring, pretending you don't know about, refusing to tune in to, as you cover your ears and close your eyes and scrunch up your face and INSIST -

That there's not a thing, there never WAS a thing, you know NOTHING about the thing and you're actually taking FUCKLOADS of impressive action thank you very much so WHO THE HELL IS MENTIONING A THING?!

Yeppppp -

THAT thing.

:)

Come on now ... no need to get upset, or sigh, or act so weary about it. I KNOW you freaking WANT to talk about it! I know you're actually DESPERATE to do so, but not just to talk, but to scream, and shout, and let it ALLL the way out, you want to bathe in it, bask in it, you want to BE it, you want to eat it and breathe it and rub it ALL OVER YOUR BODY -

Inside.

And out.

Until the thing is you and you are the thing and there is no TELLING -

Where it ends.

Nor where you begin.

THE WAY IT'S ALWAYS BEEN MEANT TO BE, actually.

So that when people look at you or meet you or in any way drink you IN, they also get the thing. You = thing, thing = you.

Everybody knows.

It's just how it is.

It's who you ARE, it's who you've ALWAYS been, it's WHAT YOU CAME HERE TO DO!

Here?

This life this earth this world.

Your flesh your blood your bones.

Your heart your soul your mind.

The ESSENCE

The SPIRIT

Of you.

It's actually the ONLY thing out of ALL the things (and by gosh do you manage to do a lot of other things!) - which could ever have BEEN a thing, considering how it's WHO YOU ARE and all.

Which really does just make you have to ask, though - (don't you think?) -

HOW ON EARTH ARE YOU MANAGING TO STAND UPRIGHT LIKE THAT WHEN YOU'RE NOT DOING THE THING THAT IS YOU AND YOU ARE IT?!

How do you keep GOING?

How are you even BREATHING?

I don't understand how it is you manage to even keep going?!

Relentlessly

Pushing forward

On the wrong fucking life

It's actually quite impressive! Or at least, it would be, if it weren't so GOD AWFUL TERRIBLE.

To see you give your life

For a Thing

And a million more

Which is not the thing, your thing, THAT thing

And when I say I don't understand how it is you just keep GOING, of COURSE I understand gorgeous, because never forget - !

I am you and you are I and the things I say to you I am really saying to ME, but only -

Always.

And sometimes I speak to a younger version of myself, to when I didn't know, how to step up, how to own it, take THAT motherfuckers, and here I am!

But sometimes?

When I talk about a thing, or about hiding, or about sabotage, or about resisting or playing small or getting to now choose to ALLOW more -

(so much more)

- I'm talking, right here, right now, yes in THIS very moment, to me.

Every blog I post

Every livestream I unleash

Every piece of this book

Every THING I create

I do it for me. Your MESSAGE, your ART, your TRUTH, the thing INSIDE of you, is first and foremost and in some ways actually ONLY -

For you.

You do know that, right? You do know it's SO not about the MONEY or the SUCCESS or the FAME or the GLORY or what-the-fuck-ever all those other things you're chasing even ARE?

(And I don't mean -

for a second -

not to chase them, want them, ask for them, and also, of course -

receive.

You get to have it ALL baby!)

It's just that ... those things aren't the reason to do THE thing, and it's also not EVER how to decide WHAT YOU SHOULD DO NEXT.

What should you do -

To make that money to grow that list to call in your tribe to monetize on purpose and hell yeah and on repeat and like WOAH?

What should you do?

WELL.

WHAT ARE YOU BEING TOLD TO DO?!

Is actually the only question

Ever

To ask

What is the message which flows through you and from you and all the way fucking over you and what is the God.Damn.THING?!

And since we're talking about it and all -

WHYYYYYYYYYYYYYYYYYYYYYYYYYYYY do you not in fact just bloody well DO it?

Oh, okay then -

You had to buy a thing.

So you can do the thing. Okay.

Or you had to learn a thing, research a thing, maybe get over a thing, before you then do THE thing? Got it ...

Or, yes, I hear you - !

You had to get READY, internally, hmmmmmm - GOOD one! Very spiritually conscious sabotage there. SMART. I see what you're doing though; JUST SO YOU KNOW ;)

OR.

YOU COULD JUST FUCKING DO THE THING.

Just like this

Just like now

Just like woah

Imperfect

Messy

Raw

Unfinished

Appalling NON-clarity around what it even actually IS, except that you know it is RIGHT because FINALLY -

- and the very moment you step into it FOR even a moment -

You can BREATHE again.

Don't you want to be able

(my darling)

to get up in the morning

(my sweet one)

and fucking BREATHE AGAIN

YOU RIDICULOUS SILLY WOMAN?!

And ALLLLLLLLLL you have to DOOOOOOOOOOOOO

Is

Do

the damn

THING!

So here is what I want to say to you suggest to you and yes, I do know, no need to tell me, that I just said 955 words of other stuff first:

You've got this.

You have permission.

You're allowed to follow what's inside of you.

It's actually the only way.

Nothing else will ever fill or satisfy you, not money, not fame, not success, not glory, not even LOVE!

Do the thing.

Do the thing.

Do the thing.

Start today.

Start today.

Start today.

I PROMISE you -

That when you give your all to live the life you deep within know you MUST?

It fucking works baby.

It flows.

And yes, it hurts and it's God awful at TIMES.

But it is, no matter the pain or the hardship which comes with it, no matter the EXCRUCIATING release you must REPEATEDLY endure -

SO.

FUCKING.

WORTH IT.

And just on a side note??? All of that ... STUFF ... you're trying too hard to GET ... and all of that MONEY ... you wish you could figure out how to receive? And all of that ... VALIDATION and AFFIRMATION and YES ... you THINK it's about and you need?

Yeah.

ALL of that comes autofuckingmatically when you first -

Do the fucking thing.

CHAPTER FIFTEEN - I BELIEVE IN PURPOSE. I BELIEVE IN CALLING. I BELIEVE IN DESTINY. I BELIEVE IN YOU.

So.

Now that I have RANTED and UNLEASHED at you, I want to talk to you, in a quiet and calm manner, about purpose.

I've been lying in bed for the past 90 minutes or so, not moving, listening to the sound of my babes sleep on either side of me, and just gazing out the window at the incredible night-time coast view, letting the weight of all that I know I must do just -

Wash over me.

Do you ever feel that way? That there's so much to do you can't possibly even begin? I wrote a post once, on an old secret blog of mine once, it's still there actually, if you know my favourite combinations of words very well you could probably find it; this one-time online journal I used to write to myself, and the blog was about how we get frozen -

In overwhelm.

At all that is in us, at all that wants out of us, at the ideas - oh!

The OH so many ideas, which just tumble from us, continually, voices, longing to be heard, messages, determined to get out, things we MUST say and do and NOW, and then -

They're gone.

The very second you don't get RIGHT THE FUCK UP and release, unleash, ALLOW it ... poof -

It floats, or it blends, or it bends, and it becomes a whisper, a shadow, a doubt in our mind, an imprint so faint you can't even tell if it was ever actually there -

If it ever even mattered -

If it was POSSIBLE to do anything with it ANYWAY, and you try to tell yourself it's okay, that one didn't matter, obviously! Or I would have done it, I would have made the post, written the blog, done the live, sounded the fucking HORN, and CLEARLY that one didn't MATTER!

But we say it -

(And you can admit it, I join as one with you right now and I admit it also, for me)

- with a slight edge of desperation, of frustration, and actually, dare I say -

of grief.

For the message that died, in that moment, because we couldn't run fast enough to catch it, because we tried to table it for even the merest of breaths.

And it's fucking sad and it's annoying, actually it's infuriating, to think, of ALL THE FANTASTIC FUCKING THINGS I COULD BE DOING IF ONLY I COULD MOVE FROM THIS PLACE OF BEING FROZEN BY ALL THE FANTASTIC FUCKING THINGS I COULD BE DOING.

You know?

You know.

And these are some of the thoughts which I allowed to wash over me, as I lay, statue like, and wondered:

What am I clinging to, because I'm scared of what the empty space would mean if I let go?

And what do I really want, from love or a man?

And what do I really want at ALL?

And what would I be DOING, if I were acting ONLY from love and alignment, if I removed the fear of loss and so therefore removed the ABILITY for fear to have any sort of a say at all?

What would I do -

Who would I be -

What would I ASK for -

And receive?

These are the things I wonder.

Most of every day, I wonder. Don't you? Don't you dig in ... don't you question ... don't you CONTINUALLY ask what it would BE like, what you would choose, NOW, if you truly knew you could have it all?

(And then ... you DO fucking go do it, choose it, think it, feel it, yes?!)

These are not idle questions to ask of oneself.

These are the questions which MUST consume us, if we are to live the life we were born for.

And then?

Well then.

We must act.

And it IS heavy, and it IS painful, and it hurts SO fucking much at times, to even THINK about the act of getting up, beginning again, every damn day and every time you pause to draw breath it's like you must BEGIN TO LABOUR ALL OVER AGAIN, but yet -

Such is the way.

Of an artist.

Of a messenger.

Of one who is called.

To screw the rules.

And who is also going to live INTO those things.

So you might well lay, for an hour or more, and allow yourself to be swept up in the WEIGHT of it all, allow the MUCHNESS of your very BEING to consume you, allow yourself to become frozen, and even begin, perhaps, to buy into the story that yes -

What you need right now is to pause.

A night off, that's it!

A day where you don't have to do the art, the unleashing, the pain, the birthing (and oh - ! how I SWORE I would never use that statement, but there it is!), a day where you can just -

Be.

And the message, screw the message, it can wait!

Except -

How can you be anything -

Except for who you indeed ARE?

You know?

You know.

And screw the message? Screw the MESSAGE? The message is EVERYTHING, we will live for it, fight for it, we breathe ONLY for it, and we WILL die for it.

You KNOW?

You know.

So, if you're to just BE, if I'm to just BE, if we are to just take a moment, a breath, a day, and pause, and rest, we need it, don't worry, it's time to just BE -

Then who the hell are we meant to, in fact, be?

If not ourselves?

Well?

Well.

Let's just fucking ADMIT, once and for all.

There IS no being without the art, the madness, the chaos, the mess, the UNLEASHING, the God.Damned.Fucking. unleashing and YES fucking ACCEPT that no matter how much you let out there will ALWAYS be more. You will NEVER be done you will be SPENT AND SPENT AND SPENT and you will spend ALL of your energy, your emotion, your soul, your breath, your LIFE -

And still.

It will keep on coming.

Like a tidal fucking wave on repeat.

Towards you.

Another message.

Another must.

Another RELEASE.

Washing over you and through you and asking you and DEMANDING of you and TELLING you to wake the fuck up and REMEMBER WHO YOU ARE.

And who you are is this:

You were born for this art.

You were born for this madness.

You were born for the mess.

You are NOT of this world.

YOU WOULDN'T FUCKING WANT TO BE.

But you WILL re-create it.

Inside.

And out.

One breath, one release, one PUSH

at a time.

Until there's no push

left

to give

And so, when you sit there -

And you lay there -

And you wonder -

How you can possibly begin when there's TOO FUCKING MUCH and you're SCARED, so damn SCARED of losing hold of what must come out, so you FREEZE, and you try to cling to it, to capture it, to not breathe because if you don't move a muscle or even your soul then SURELY YOU WON'T LOSE IT -

Just remember -

Who you fucking are.

What you came here to do.

That the ONLY way is to do the work.

Do the work.

Do the work.

That EVERYTHING you are about is the work.

The work.

The work.

That everything ELSE is merely a distraction, as brief as possible, from the work.

The work.

The work.

And then?

GO AND DO THE FUCKING WORK.

My daughter told me -

That today in school there was no learning. The last day of school, how fun!

We didn't have to learn ANYTHING today, she said.

We just did art.

And I wanted to cry in fury at the BULLSHIT that is being re-cycled out there. How even at the most CAREFULLY chosen of schools, and I do in fact LOVE that school, where they teach manifestation, and yoga daily, and beliefs by choice, and tuning in, there is still learning -

And then there is art.

And I RAGED, internally, and out loud I indignantly stated, with much perfect grammar, that art is TOO learning, at which my 7-year old looked at me with that eye-rolling 'here go the old folks again' look -

"No it's not! Art is FUN! It's not learning!"

- and off she ran.

(A conversation.

May be had :))

But as she ran to play, I RAGED some more, and I ROARED inside of me at this RIDICULOUS THING THE WORLD DOES OF PUSHING

the creators

DOWN

And I thought -

You can't make money from your art?! It's not learning? It's not growth? It doesn't matter?

Okay.

MAYBE IT'S EVEN FUCKING TRUE, who knows?

{Well ... me. That's who}

But either way, let me ask you:

CAN YOU FUCKING BREATHE WITHOUT IT?

And even if you can inhale -

In little gasps and breaths -

Then answer me this:

How can you even be?

If being is not being who you are?

I believe in purpose.

I believe in destiny.

I believe in calling.

I believe that art, and message, and truth is the WAY.

I believe in you.

CHAPTER SIXTEEN - YOU'RE A WARRIOR QUEEN, A SUPERSTAR, BORN TO SHINE AND LEAD - GET OVER YOURSELF AND START SHOWING UP LIKE IT! -

I want to tell you a story, a secret, a download, a truth, it's a WHISPER from my soul to yours except that I feel like the whispering thing isn't working so well right now so I'm just going to SHOUT it.

And I don't know why it's not occurred to me until just now that we have to have some words about this, you and I.

That there is ass to be kicked. Yes. It's time. Mostly yours, although you KNOW that ain't true, 'cause if I'm kicking your butt or PREACHING to its fine self (insert odd mental image of me preaching to your butt), then I'm ALWAYS first and foremost kicking mine, because one thing we know for SURE is that the message which comes through?

Comes through firstly for YOU.

Yours for you, and mine for me.

So if I find that I feel the need to YELL at you, to RANT at you, to hold a mirror up in front of you and ask you WHO THE HELL YOU THINK YOU'RE SHOWING UP AS, 'cause it ain't that true next level LEADER | STAR you, then clearly I feel a need to look in the God damn mirror myself.

Which I do.

And I shall.

Always.

Again.

But before I yell before I rant before I tell you a story, a secret, a download, a TRUTH, can I tell you this?

You're so fucking beautiful.

You shine from within.

You are SO clearly born for it that it's evident to EVERYONE all around you.

You have something about you that is truly REGAL -

You carry yourself in a way which STANDS OUT.

There is POWER INSIDE OF YOU and as much as you do seem to be trying oddly hard to contain it, it's seeping out of you -

From every pore of you -

And it's letting people know:

Listen.

Sit up.

Pay attention when THIS one speaks.

You shine like a WARRIOR Queen, a superstar, like one who came here to MAGNETIZE and to unleash a message which will impact MILLIONS.

And you know it, I don't have to tell you all of this stuff, do I? It's only been inside of you since BEFORE TIME BEGAN. So, if you sit up a little straighter and prouder or you feel affirmed from my words or you feel that whisper and flutter of excitement inside of you as your soul says YES, then GOOD, but also, seriously girl -

When do you think you might like to just turn the dial up to full fucking bright?

Or is it that you're more so just planning to leak out little bits of your light, here and there, when it builds up so much that you can't not, when it bubbles out and over.

Little patches of light and truth and power that you leave around town all behind you, a trail of transformative breadcrumbs, but yet when people follow it and they get to you, you:

Well.

Let's just be fucking honest, yeah? Why not?!

You hold them at arm's length.

You find yourself freezing, a little, in fear.

You turn somewhat STATUE-like, at times.

And slowly -

Sneakily -

So that nobody can really notice or know if you were EVEN THERE IN THE FIRST PLACE -

You turn your light down

down

down

until it fades to black

And oh SURE, you might still be showing UP, you're posting shit! You're SAYING things! You are doing the WORK ...

Kind of.

Except -

NOT FUCKING REALLY AT ALL, not the discipline, not the consistency, not the relentless and obsessed will-not-back down day in and day out of it that you'd have if you were ACTUALLY fully committed to your vision.

At the end of the day you've either DONE THE WORK YOU NEEDED TO DO to be the TRUE you, and step INTO the light, BE centre stage where you SHOULD be -

Or you've not.

There is no in between.

It's black and white.

Kind of like -

Christian, or not. Pregnant, or not. You can't say - kind of, sort of, partly.

So, which is it? When you look in, when you look OUT, when you look back on your DAY, your WEEK, and ultimately the future you are RIGHT NOW STEPPING INTO through your actions, your energy, your way of being YOU, are you SHINING YOUR LIGHT AS IT SHOULD BE?

Or not?

I said I had to tell you something, and I suppose I could eventually get there and perhaps I've already said it without saying it, but let me be clear:

PLENTY are born for it.

EVERYBODY has a gift to share.

Everybody has a MESSAGE, and there are many of us who came here to BE A LIGHT FOR OTHERS.

But there are a few -

A VERY few -

And I speak all of the time about being the 1% within the 1%, and THAT IS WHO WE ARE! In this community we are FULLY the 1% within the 1% of entrepreneurs, creators, leaders, artists, performers, REVOFUCKINGLUTIONARIES who came here to UNLEASH.

It's a given - !

If you're here -

That you have it inside of you to MAKE millions, IMPACT millions, change the world and also HAVE IT ALL on your terms.

But there are a FEW -

And here is where I speak to you, I whisper, and I SHOUT, the SECRET ... and it's not a secret in the normal sense, it's a secret in the sense that you don't DARE TO LOOK AT IT, mostly -

Or maybe even at all.

And the secret, the story, the message, the download, for YOU, from ME, today:

Some of us are the 1% within the 1% within the 1% to INFINITY and we are the TRUE leaders.

Performers.

Visionaries.

MESSENGERS.

We are connected and FULLY tapped in.

To God.

To the Universe.

To the MESSAGE.

And we ACTUALLY ARE GOING TO CHANGE THE WORLD, it's not just a thing to SAY.

We are the leaders of the leaders, we were born PURELY to message and unleash and to SHINE.

And we have a fucking responsibility to live into that.

This is what I see, when I look at you.

A reflection of ME, in you.

A TRUE warrior Queen, a true star, one who really IS not of this world, but yet we came here to SHINE IN IT.

And I also see this:

You're not showing the fuck up.

You're not shining at even 5% of what you've got baby.

You're allowing fear to be the guiding light more often than truth.

AND YOU CAN CHANGE THAT AT ANY MOMENT IN TIME. Like right.fucking.now.

And I wonder:

What would the world see of you, from this day forward, do you think -?

If you decided to just remove emotion, fear, uncertainty,

And lead the fucking charge like you actually had accepted -

The role God gave you.

Think about it.

And then draw a line in the sand.

Because being born for it? Has NOTHIN' to do with whether you ever do it.

You either are, fully, NOW, or the brutal truth is you likely never will.

Rip the fucking Band-Aid gorgeous.

AND SHINE SO BRIGHTLY THAT WE CAN BARELY LOOK AT YOU -

But yet NEVER turn away from you.

Screw the rules.

Just do you.

CHAPTER SEVENTEEN DO YOU LISTEN WHEN YOUR SOUL SPEAKS TO YOU?

There are so many times, each and every day, too many to count, when the message, the truth, the download, the RELEASE wants to come through us, and we simply turn away.

Do you notice this? I know you DO it ... it's the human way. To resist doing the work which must be done, and instead turn into everything BUT. So, I'm not asking whether you DO this, whether you resist, whether you dance away from the SOUL work which would allow you to step deeper and perhaps even fully (is there such a thing?!) into flow and the life you were BORN for.

I'm asking:

Do you notice?

Do you ALLOW yourself to notice the moments, the breaths, the whisper, the call of your soul, telling you:

Stop everything.

Turn away.

Ignore the world.

Let it fade to grey.

And go WITHIN my dear, go within, again.

Do you listen, when your soul speaks?

Or are you too busy for that, you can't do what your soul commands now, there's TOO much to do and you are VERY Important, don't you know!

As you continue to give

Your life

To everything

But what it was formed for

I find myself continually in a battle of sorts, an inner war, between the me who can be OH so reactive, to the world around, or to her own changing emotions, or simply to the Things Which MUST Be Done.

The God Damn things

Which must be done

And so I might come stumbling out of a hot yoga class, back onto the grimy and dusty and oh so beautiful Bali streets, feeling shaky like a baby deer, just learning to walk, because hot damn that was a POWERFUL one, the sweat flowing in rivers from me, the CLEANSING so deep it left me trembling, feeling as though I was stripped back to my soul and I fully shed -

A new layer.

And I am awakened, I am raw, I am stripped bare, and I feel connected to ALL that matters and is true, and yet -

And yet.

(And I know that you do this too)

It's so EASY to then slip straight back into conscious thought, isn't it?

The mask back on.

Shoulders squared.

There is work to be done, emails to be responded to, people who seem to have their entire life revolving around just having meaningless banter and fun, and you find yourself at times fascinated by whether they've discovered some secret that you don't know, but mostly just irritated -

That so few seem to fucking GET what life should be about.

That they don't get or seem to want to even KNOW about this DEEP, deep work which just won't stop flowing out; how when there is this there is only this and NOTHING else matters, but YET -

There you go.

Again.

Slowly but surely coming back into being fully present with the HUMAN people. And instead of sitting down and continuing the deepening of the CLEANSE, the release, and what must come out of you, instead of remaining one foot in and one foot out of the world, living really just INSIDE of you even as your body walks around, shows up, appears to be SOMEWHAT present and in attendance -

You become.

Once more.

One of them.

And today I decided ... another little break free, of the chains which continually seek to bind me, you, those like US, back into being like THEM ... I decided that actually, no.

Even though I have already written several thousands of words this morning.

Even though I have ambled slowly, and with limbs heavy in beautiful languor and blood thick like honey, into my day -

Dreaming

And journaling

And wondering

And I've taken already SO much time for ME, for the things that MAKE me me, and normally I would ... I SHOULD ... now sit down and do the fucking THINGS, that actually -

No.

Thank you.

I think I'll sit here.

As the sweet Indonesian man dries and straightens and all but individually and strand by strand polishes my hair -

And I will not check in.

I will not respond.

I will not JUMP, to their commands, their friendly inquiries, their questions, their asking -

"Can Kat come out and play?!"

Well, sometimes I can, but no, not right now.

I'm going in.

I'm going in.

I'm going in.

There is something I must say to YOU; my soul is telling me.

There is writing to be done.

There is PURPOSE work to be unleashed.

And so here I am. Writing, once more, something about nothing. Pushing away, once more, that part of my CRITICAL mind, the HUMAN mind, the BUSY, busy bee mind, the LOGICAL shit, which tries to tell me:

THIS DOESN'T EVEN MAKE ANY SENSE!

You're just RAMBLING! Where do you think you're even GOING with all of this, OH, you think you can be a WRITER, a real one?

And I think:

Shut the fuck up.

I am who I say I am.

I am who I SHOW myself to be.

I'm a fucking writer baby, and when my soul says to write, I WRITE.

And as it so HAPPENS (I say to that DEVIL who taunts and teases me) the fact that I have REPEATEDLY had the God damn DISCIPLINE to not do all the OTHER things, the BUSY work things, the things I supposedly SHOULD do in order to stay on top, get ahead, or even just keep up -

And that I've instead repeatedly turned in, tuned in, listened in and ACTED from within -

Has in fact allowed me to build a freaking EMPIRE, of multiple millions made and also multiple millions IMPACTED.

Because I repeatedly ignored what I HAD to do.

And I did what I get to do.

And I wonder ...

What do you think might happen for YOU, if you were to tune in like this, if when your soul spoke to you, from this day forward -

You listened.

Just an idea ...

CHAPTER EIGHTEEN - WHAT IT MEANS TO SCREW THE RULES, AND JUST DO YOU

I'm still so conscious of the need to write something that gives you a PROCESS to dive into.

I feel that this is what you want ... yes? I don't know. Maybe you want it, maybe you don't. Perhaps, as I hoped would be the case, you are simply carried away with the knowledge and the TRUTH, of what my soul is saying to yours.

Perhaps, as you read my ramblings, which go nowhere, and everywhere, and anywhere, but certainly are not METHODICALLY put together, something within you has awakened, and whispered -

Yes.

Things are going to change now.

I know it.

I choose it.

AND SO IT IS.

AND you have no idea what it will BE, or HOW, or where to even start (start here; right here!), but you just know it WILL.FUCKING.HAPPEN.

And if that is ALL you take from this book, then gorgeous one, it is EVERYTHING I wanted you to.

I wanted you to wake up.

I wanted you to remember.

I wanted you to tune in.

I wanted you to fucking CONNECT again, with your SOUL, and tell it -

Yes.

From here on out.

I WILL fucking listen, and also -

Act.

That's what I want and pray for you.

So is my wish.

And perhaps I do this more so for ME, because I tell myself YOU want this, or my book agent wants this, or WHAT IF NONE OF THIS MAKES SENSE WITHOUT THIS, but maybe it's all a lie and it's just my OWN insecurities prompting me to write THIS piece, but NOW -

The how.

Of screwing the rules.

And doing you.

1) Shut the fuck up, and listen

Listen to who? To YOU of course! Listen in and ask yourself -

Who you are meant to be? What truly matters? What you WANT.

2) Decide

Next, you simply decide. Yes, I will be that person. Yes, I'll chase and allow and create that. Yes, it is DONE.

3) Commit

Deciding isn't quite enough. You've got to also COMMIT.

I commit to what I desire.

I commit to what is done.

I commit to what I know I MUST.

I commit and I will do WHAT it takes, no matter what it takes, until it takes!

Okay!

4) Be fucking clear, then ask

Before you carry on another STEP, check in -

Are you being clear on what you want, desire, know you must? If you're not CRYSTAL fucking clear, as best as you can be, then don't be surprised if you don't get what you want!

You'll get what you ASK for and expect.

Ask properly :)

5) RELEASE RELEASE RELEASE

In order to manifest, you MUST release.

Release being attached to the outcome.

Release the idea that you have to HAVE it.

Release that you NEED it; you don't.

YES, you can decide it's done, and fully fucking mean it.

But, you're not God. You don't know the most aligned path. Have FAITH that what will be is meant to be.

And let go.

6) Fuck the HOW

Don't.

Worry.

About.

How.

As SOON as you fuss about the 'how' of getting there, you're no longer focused on the THERE.

Which means ... you'll go somewhere else. You go where your focus is. Don't focus on how!

7) Surrender to the now and what IS

This is another layer of releasing.

Letting go.

TRUSTING.

Having FAITH.

And accepting that what IS, is what is meant to be. All you need to do aside from this?

8) Take.Inspired.Action.

Your only real JOB each day, aside from tuning in and being honest about what you see, is to take inspired and aligned action.

That's it.

Towards your goals? Yes, but really what it means is to, moment by moment ask - what is the best use of THIS MOMENT RIGHT HERE.

And then DO what comes UP for you.

Trust, remember? And faith.

That's it.

Onwards!

CHAPTER NINETEEN - THE THING WHICH YOU GET FASCINATED AND EXCITED BY IN OTHERS, IS THE THING YOU SHOULD DO

Pay attention, and listen closely, because what I'm about to tell you could VERY well not only stop you from creating the wrong life, but could also save you a fuckload of money, time, energy, emotion, your LIFE and in doing so provide you absolute time, freedom and FUCK YES certainty to pursue the Thing Which You Were Born to Do Yet Refuse to Take Ownership Over.

And the best part? You'll know how to apply this to YOU as soon as you read my story and philosophy here –

Quite recently, I walked away from something that sounded insanely seductive, amazing, appealing, and was maybe EVERYTHING I've ever wanted or certainly everything a driven girl wanting to be seen and heard could dream of.

At the time I tore myself apart from the inside out trying to figure out whether it was my GUT telling me to walk away or whether fear and self-sabotage was trying to have its wily way with me again and I should WOMAN THE FUCK UP AND FOLLOW THROUGH.

You know when something is a REALLY big decision, and you're really caught up in emotion around it, and you can't seem to just KNOW, as you so often do in so many less important areas?

Yeah ... that.

I analysed this thing till the cows came home, went to sleep, and went back out again for the next day.

I went back and forth with my team, my best friends, my journal, and even my blow dry girl (obvs; the woman knows everything about me!).

And still I couldn't figure it out.

There were SO many reasons this was a GOOD thing, an AMAZING thing, EVERYthing, in fact, but yet the YES I needed to give just wouldn't come out of me. Instead I found myself picking over details, analysing whats and ifs, and tossing and turning through the night as I drove myself insane wondering if really, I was just being a CRYBABY about stepping outside of my comfort zone.

Sometimes when you think that maybe your gut is saying NO, really what's happening is you're just anxious about going through the inevitable pain that comes with GROWTH. They don't call it growing pains for naught!

Anyway –

To be perfectly honest with you, even though I made my decision some time back, it's still been something I wrestled with. Did I choose WRONG? Did I screw it UP? Am I CRAZY, to say NO to that?!

And then, this. And the reason for this chapter –

This morning I was reading a blog written by James Altucher (my favourite blogger and second favourite writer!), and in passing he mentioned John Grisham. He said –

"One time I was visiting a hedge fund that managed John Grisham's money. They told me, 'Every time John Grisham writes a book we get another $20 million to invest.'"

Straight away I stopped reading the blog and began writing this, five minutes ago. Because what HIT me in that moment was not that John Grisham is clearly marketable AF, and not even that I've obsessively read everything he ever wrote since I was a teenager, but more so that I right away felt that RUSH inside of me when his name was mentioned.

And the RUSH is partly because yes, I'm a John fan, and yes, I know enough of his back story to know he was knocked back as an author and FOLLOWED THE FUCK THROUGH till he made it, but mostly –?

It was the rush I feel whenever my soul gets wind of somebody succeeding in a world-famous and without question OVERT manner as an author.

I get the same rush when I think of my client, Lili St Germain, who said to me on our first conversation maybe three years ago that she wanted to be a full-time best-selling author and who five months later had quit her job and made $100k self-publishing on Amazon, who then got OFFERED (as you do!) a 6-figure book deal from Harper Collins ... they came to HER ... and who is now a USA Today best-selling author! I keep her books on my bookstand and I get EXCITED each time I see them, in a way that transcends even hearing a client did a $100k launch, made their first million, got on TV, etc!

You know what else you'll find on my bedside table, actually, my two bedside tables?

Piles.

And piles.

Of books.

Lili's books.

John Grisham's books.

Jeffrey Archer books (if you haven't read Jeffrey Archer and you call yourself a lover of writing GET YOUR SHIT TOGETHER ... and put aside a spare month or so as you won't want to put them down)

Piles and piles of personal development books of all sorts and shapes and sizes.

And about 50 kids' books too

I actually don't even know how I ended up with so many books on my little tables; I swear there were only about four on each a few months ago and now there seems to be a leaning tower of Pisa-esque situation going on either side.

Over the past few years, it's safe to say I've read several million words of online success stories, case studies, and invaluable advice on all areas of BUSINESS and success in general.

Wanna know what I remember, what I would go back to?

When Tim Ferriss wrote about how to get a 7-figure book deal.

When James Altucher wrote (multiple times) about how to self-publish, why to self-publish over anything else.

When he interviewed Steve Scott about how Steve makes \$40k (more now) a month self-publishing on Amazon.

When I then obsessively searched everything on Steve, listened to all his podcast interviews, purchased a program from him so I could get the free 30-minute 1:1 he offered as a fast-action bonus, wrote down EVERYTHING he said to do.

When I first read *Write. Publish. Repeat.*, then obsessively looked up and followed everything those three guys do.

When I first came across Mark Messick, who had major self-published success at sixteen, obsessively read everything of his and about him.

When I first heard of Amanda Hocking and obsessively read everything about HER insane self-published success.

When I first encountered John Locke, read all HIS stuff obsessively (awesome books btw!) and also read his book on how he created his self-published success, and then forced my Dad, and everybody else I could influence on reading at the time, to read it too.

When I first came across Tom Corson-Knowles who was then making $10k/month self-publishing on Amazon; more now.

When I then did Tom's Udemy course and would listen and be inspired and imagine that being me while I did my cardio at the gym.

When I then paid him $1k for a one-hour session and wrote down EVERYTHING he said to do.

And so many other stories, of so many other writers, of those who said FUCK it and decided to follow their WRITING dream, and do it their way, and then they MADE it.

Want to know something funny? In all of the above situations, as I dreamed and made notes and imagined what it would be like, I already HAD a million-dollar online business!! I wasn't exactly sitting on my haunches not achieving, but in the moments where I read about somebody making it big as an author, about somebody publishing loads of books, it was like nothing else I've ever done or ever will do mattered.

Do you ever feel that way? Is there something which, when you think about it, COMPLETELY captures your attention and all of a sudden you don't give a single flying fuck about ANYTHING and you MUST KNOW EVERYTHING ABOUT THAT TOPIC OR THE PERSON WHO ACHIEVED AT IT.

What is it that's coming to mind for you right now?

What is the THING, which you find you just HAVE to delve into, when you hear about somebody doing it?

What are the things you REMEMBER, from all of the stuff you've read, learned, absorbed these past few years?

What stands out for you?

This is the thing it's really about for you, I can promise you that.

The thing which you're excited by in others and obsessively want to know HOW they freaking DID it, is the THING YOU'RE MEANT TO DO.

And the DANGEROUS trap so many of us fall into, is to put our time, our energy, our money, our emotion, our LIFE, into pursuing something that looks very much like this thing.

That is CLOSELY related to this thing.

And that perhaps, in a roundabout way, could even GET us to this thing.

But yet it's not the thing.

Want to know something REALLY weird and funny, which just occurred to me? For some reason I never get as excited, in fact I never even pay attention, when somebody new hits the NYT list!! This is bizarre to me, as it's 'always' been my dream to be on that list.

But no, I can't say I've ever sat down and obsessively read stories of how people made it. I definitely want the goal ... but it's an ego goal. There's nothing wrong with ego goals! So long as they're not followed at the expense of SOUL goals. And the soul goal, for me, is the writing. Of books. MANY books. ENDLESS books. And the building, of an empire of them, on my terms.

How about you?

And then – are you DOING it?

Are you making SPACE for it? Even thirty minutes a day to pursue this DREAM which you were BORN for?! The only reason I completed my first book, was because I started to put aside thirty minutes a day to write. Twenty-five for the writing and five for recalibrating or doing follow up tasks relevant to the writing.

I know from hard-won experience that COMMONLY what happens, even for us driven folks, perhaps ESPECIALLY for us, is that we put our big dream, the thing we really want, up on a pedestal.

And we tell ourselves:

That's too hard.

That's not for me.

I don't know how.

It's scary!

I'm not GOOD enough!

But meanwhile we try and move HEAVEN AND FUCKING EARTH to do a whole bunch of other stuff which actually is, in a logical sense, just as hard or requires just as much effort, but yet because it's not the thing we REALLY want, we don't have the same resistance around it and we're just pragmatic about it.

Well, here's an idea:

What if, today, you decided to take that big one-day dream down off its motherfucking shelf, dust it off, and simply apply yourself to it.

In a very PRACTICAL and non-romantic one foot in front of the other sort of a way.

Do you think –

That if you dedicated thirty minutes a day to pursuing your ACTUAL thing –

That one day people might be reading about how YOU did it?

Or would you prefer to stay on the outside, looking in, achieving a whole bunch of stuff it was NEVER MEANT TO BE ABOUT, 'cause hey –

You're a go-getter, baby! You get shit DONE! Just not the actual shit because that's harrrdddddddd!

Go get the thing you were always meant to get gorgeous.

And you know what else? Do it starting TODAY.

PS

I totally thought I was going to put together something COMPLETELY different in this chapter (planned, even!) for you, but over the past day or two the message has been coming to me VERY clearly, and with an increasingly loud LISTEN TO ME sort of tone.

RESISTANCE baby.

It will KILL you, if you allow it to.

Every day, I am reminded in some form of what I've been able to achieve and create in my business, my fitness, my LIFE, as a result of getting TF over the RESISTANCE which had previously, in that area, held me back.

Wanna know the number one reason you WON'T ever press play, or live your dreams?

You damn straight KNOW it's got nothing to do with whether or not you CAN ...!

It's because you don't create the motherfucking habit.

It's because you don't create the DISCIPLINE.

It's because, straight up, you don't do the WORK, but what THAT is really about is you listen to the voice which tells you it's too HARD, you're not READY, you're maybe not GOOD enough, and besides – you don't FEEL like it!

Well, I for one have had ENOUGH! I've learned over and over again that if I commit to something and create the HABIT I can achieve ANYTHING, and I know that's true for you TOO.

But I also know how damn hard it is to GET moving when resistance has you bound, trapped, scared, and TRULY believing your own BS. Somehow day after day after week after week after month passes by and you can't even quite understand how you got THIS much older and you've still not done it.

I’m so passionate about seeing you press play, live your purpose, make shit TRULY happen in all areas of your life.

Get ready to press fucking play, the way you’ve always SAID you would. Now that we've discussed HOW, let's talk about WHAT.

I've spoken to you repeatedly about the THING.

I so believe in the THING, for YOU, that there IS one, and that you do.know.what.it.is.

I know, I know, I'm VERY heavy handed with the periods between words for emphasis thing. So what, I like it!

I'm also very liberal with the discussion around the THING. It's a passion, what can I say?!

Wanna know the good news? I know how you can know what the thing is. So there!

But what about -

Getting it actually done?

CHAPTER TWENTY -DON'T TELL ME WHAT TO DO, MAN!

My son, who is now coming up to four years old, is my second baby, my MIRACLE baby. I spent a good deal of the second half of his pregnancy hospitalised with a placenta percreta-escaping placenta! ... and having increasingly serious haemorrhaging ... it was a journey, that's for sure! Anyway, my son has this thing he says, where you can't help but laugh even though it's mostly kinda naughty, which is this -

"Don't tell me what to do, man!"

And it's just fucking FUNNY, and he'll say it even if you're NOT telling him what to do, and he has this real BOSS baby attitude about it, with his crazy curly surfer locks, and I'll say back to him - "Hey! I DIDN'T even tell you what to do, but if I wanted to I would!!"

It makes me think of how I feel when I receive even a HINT that somebody might be trying to put me under command, tell me what's up or that there are things I have to do.

"I don't gotta do ANYTHING!", my mind shrieks.

"And I won't!"

And I know there is definitely a bit of a trigger-happy response that goes on there, when I REMOTELY feel that somebody is questioning me, but you know what? Fuck it! I bet you're the same, and whilst we could totally tell ourselves to 'grow up', or think before we talk, etc, you know WHAT?

Being like this is what makes you like THIS.

If you're going to say a big fuck you to the RULES, then it's also going to mean being willing to stand UP for yourself, your beliefs, and what you know INSIDE of you is right.

So, YES -

You may feel you REPEATEDLY have to insist on stomping your foot and you want all of LIFE to conform and bend to you, doing things YOUR way, ONLY. But you GET TO ACTUALLY CREATE THAT.

So, stand firm.

Be true.

DON'T BACK DOWN.

And when they tell you how to be you?

Well ...

You know what to do, DON'T you?!

Fuck.

That.

Shit.

CHAPTER TWENTY ONE - LOCK IN YOUR VISION, FUCK THE "HOW", SURRENDER THE WHOLE PROCESS, EVEN THE OUTCOME! -

Let's talk more about this process of 'fuck the how', and SURRENDER.

The further I travel down the path of creating my reality and living my dreams, in every aspect of business and life, the more I notice how much time I lost along the way, how hard I made it on myself, how much I worried about SO many things which just didn't matter.

They didn't matter in the end.

And they actually didn't even matter in the moment!

These were just the fear-driven or conditioned into me "shoulds", ideas of what is right or how it must be, or, in many cases, simply me blindly following others who were also blindly following others who were, well -

You get the idea.

And I suppose it IS one way to approach it all, isn't it?

Set a goal ... make a plan ... said plan obviously to be dependent upon the 'right' ways to do so, and also with the underlying belief that things take TIME ... come at a COST ... that you can only ascend in some sort of logical sequence ... etc ... and then of course you are supposed to FOLLOW said plan ...

And yes, it CAN work, certainly DOES work, for many people on lots of different things, but I don't know about you ... for me? I was just never that good at following a fucking plan.

I just didn't seem to be able to STICK to the damn thing, not even with the best of intentions!

And even back in school days ... I just always decided:

This is the outcome I want (basically: the best possible outcome!)

And I'm gonna get it

And thank you but NO thank you, I'm actually NOT going to be able to go ahead and do that whole 'do it by the book' way of getting it ... 'cause, well, long story short?

I kinda can't be fucked.

Never could be, actually, with rules or processes!

And still can't!

But yet somehow ... some way... since as far back as I can recall ... I ALWAYS got the freaking outcome I wanted!

I was always top of the class.

I always got the 'stuff' I wanted.

I always got the job or gig I decided.

It even worked with boys, and then men :)

So, what gives, right? Was I just LUCKY? Blessed by the Gods? Or somehow getting away with something I shouldn't have been; cheating the system?!

Do YOU feel that way, when you 'get' or achieve stuff where you haven't actually done the work that you're SUPPOSEDLY meant to do?

And if you do ... as I have often felt over the years ... feel guilty or somehow bad about it ... has it ever occurred to you that maybe we all just learned the wrong SHIT, about how to succeed in life, how to get what you want, how to NOW live your every dream?

The truth is that once you KNOW the truth, about what it really takes to receive something ... anything ... no matter how big the thing ... that old way of doing things just seems fucking RIDICULOUS!!

I don't know whether to laugh or cry when I see people still caught up in it ... and believing the dogma so whole-heartedly it seems pointless to try and state otherwise ... all we can do is live by EXAMPLE. I feel roughly as though it's like somebody still believing FULLY that the earth is flat ... you just feel SORRY for them, but if they really, really, believe it then there's not that much you can do about it!

And really, my role here is not to try and 'save' people whose ears and hearts are closed to REALITY, anyway. Nor is yours, I would imagine.

What we're here to DO, as messengers, is to live purposefully and be the light we know we are called to be, follow what we know inside of us is true and REAL, and in so doing help those who are like-minded to be empowered to follow what is inside of THEM.

Which means that when it comes to all of THIS stuff, the most important thing I can do to guide or mentor YOU, is to follow what I KNOW is true, even when I find it scary or at times I EVEN question my faith!!

But question or not, fear or not, and despite the fact that yes of COURSE I fall into the old 'earth is flat' way of doing things, pushing shit relentlessly up a hill and worrying about HOW, here is what I know for SURE:

The path to success, to receiving, to achieving, ANYTHING, is simple.

Lock in the vision.

Give yourself permission to own and CLAIM that baby, do so over and over again daily, faith means you keep asking and moving forward even though you can't SEE how, and speaking of that -

FUCK the how, you don't need to know how, yours is simply to confess to the vision and accept what is being shown to you, nobody who actually knows anything real about success ever said you have to know how!

You must also SURRENDER the entire process, keep focused on the outcome and let the process or path take you wherever it needs, oh and one more thing:

If you're really serious about this stuff and you mean it, then you ALSO surrender the outcome.

WE SPOKE ABOUT THAT.

It IS fucking critical, okay?!

When you release, you release into "this or something better / more aligned"

Because ultimately the ONLY outcome we desire is flow, happiness, a purposeful and fulfilling life, or whatever your version of that is.

So as much as you might desire or REALLY think you need ANY particular thing, there is not a SINGLE thing you actually do HAVE to have.

Everything you need is inside of you.

EVERYTHING.

God-given and heaven sent since before you began.

Which means ... EVERYthing you allow or receive in life, is not only absolutely yours for the asking, it's also just a sweet BONUS. The cherry on top of living a life completely whole.

And that life?

Is the one you'll find in your soul.

Which we also spoke about :)

CHAPTER TWENTY TWO - MAGIC IS YOUR NATURAL STATE

Do you ever find yourself just feeling absolutely AWED at how deep your powers and natural magic run?

It's astonishing to me how readily we forget this stuff, or I suppose - push it away, don't listen because it's scary, and maybe wrong.

When really? It's just your natural fucking state.

It's not a big deal.

You have INHERENT magical and psychic powers.

Some people learn to access them more than others; for some people part of their CALLING is to access and use them, but for each of us, and yes that includes YOU, they're there.

They exist.

No point pretending otherwise! And kind of foolish, if you think about it, to not just USE them, to, you know -

Make life easier, better, more in flow, more as it SHOULD be.

A silly little thing this morning reminded me just how true this is. Most mornings, I come and write at a cafe that's about a 5-minute walk from my place. Half the time, I drive here, as I'm then going directly somewhere else afterwards. Only problem is - it's a busy street; a busy neighbourhood and always risky as to whether I'll get a park, or whether I'll end up having to backtrack further back even than my own apartment garage to find one!

Today, I thought I should walk for this reason ... but I had all my gym gear already and couldn't be bothered going down to the car to drop it off then coming back OUT of the car basement again - I wanted to drive, so I could just be on my way after I write! As I went down in the lift from my building, a little voice inside me said -

"It's okay. You'll park right out the front anyway."

I heard it, and (of course!) believed it, but then forgot. As I drove up not too far away from the cafe there was a car space at the end of the street; normally I would take it right away before it gets snapped up, but then I remembered:

"Oh, that's right! I'm going to park right out the front"

I kept driving.

My park was there - 'pole position!' - waiting for me.

Of COURSE.

And as I pulled the car in, even though I DID feel 'of course' about it because I BELIEVE IN MAGIC ... and just intuitive power, really! ... I also had to shake my head at myself.

Why do I let so many things be so HARD, when I already know the answer?

Why do I do every possible thing to figure shit out based on something OUTSIDE of me, when I could just ask within -

Listen within -

And tune the fuck in!

It's so ... SILLY. I say with a smile, because I'm not hard on myself about it; more so ... BEMUSED. You know?

And I wonder:

What do you imagine would be OH so different and OH so perfect already, in your life, if you simply allowed yourself to access your NATURAL MAGICAL POWERS more readily? Or, God forbid, maybe even just ALL the time?!

Coming from a Christian background, and STILL identifying myself as Christian, I can tell you - my DEFAULT thought process is to feel anxious about this sort of stuff. It must be WRONG! It must be BAD! I should be SCARED and turn away from this sort of stuff!

And then I remember:

GOD is all about us USING THE FREAKING POWERS HE GAVE US!

GOD gave me - and you! - NATURAL intuition!

Now, you don't have to use the word MAGIC if you don't want to ... I must say, that word brings up ALL sorts of 'scary evil bad devil' shit for me ... and hence I DELIBERATELY FUCKING USE - and defuse - it, anyway.

Because all we're talking about here is your natural and even HUMAN AF state.

I speak all the time about being 'superhuman', having superpowers, and a lot of people really align with the idea of being 'special' for accessing higher consciousness stuff, collective energy, etc ... and it IS special, but you know what?

It's also very hum-fucking-drum, in the sense that we were ALL BORN WITH THESE POWERS.

Call 'em powers, call 'em gifts, call it your calling, call it what you WILL, but part of the HUMAN experience is accessing superhuman knowledge, and also things - MANY things! - we can't understand.

So, to turn your back on magic, to say no to listening to inner guidance, and also to not actively ASK your inner self for truths and wisdom is, well, it's the EQUIVALENT to having legs -

And not using them.

Because - OMG! - it must be WRONG to just be able to MOVE YOURSELF AROUND THE EARTH ANYTIME YOU WANT!

It really is fucking OUTRAGEOUS, if you think about it, and I feel outraged now, thinking about it, how so many of us have been conditioned to believe that USING THE GIFTS GOD GAVE US IS WRONG.

I don't say this REMOTELY to rail against the church, by the way, because ultimately, I choose my own perceptions and interpretations of things, and also - the more I think about it, the more I remember being taught IN church to listen in!

To that still small voice.

To that unspoken wisdom.

To God speaking through you.

And simply to what your HEART, your SOUL, your CELLS know to be true.

What I find FASCINATING is not so much the concept of inner guidance and that what you get told from inside of you is ALWAYS true, but more so that so many of us DO ALREADY KNOW THIS STUFF and yet we fail to use it.

We might use it when it makes itself KNOWN to us, when it pops up and taps us on the shoulder so to speak, but how many of us actively take time and space each day to simply listen in, and channel FROM within, the truths about what we then get to do?

I mean, sure -

I get that you're busy; you've a million things to do, you've got places to go and people to see and goals to fucking HIT, and maybe once you get to that next level you can make time for all this spiritual stuff, go woo-woo for a bit, or maybe go spend a fucking week in the jungle and pat yourself on the back for being all superhuman and shit, feel like SUCH a freakin' badass because you did something 'next level' and cool ...

OR.

I mean REALLY.

OR ... YOU COULD JUST FUCKING ACCESS THOSE POWERS ANYTIME.

Any place.

DAILY.

Because WHY THE FUCK WOULD YOU WALK AROUND EACH DAY NOT USING WHAT'S SO READILY AVAILABLE TO YOU?

NOT accessing your spiritual powers daily IS the same as not using your LIMBS daily. Imagine, if the trendy thing was to just go away on retreat once or twice a year to use your arms and legs! And then people came back all awestruck at just how much more FREEDOM and STRENGTH they had, how much more they could allow in to their lives because of this special time away!

Haha. But SERIOUSLY. That's what I see going on here! Everybody getting caught the fuck up in GOING somewhere or TAKING something or having to go through a special one-time RITUAL in order to access GOD and higher CONSCIOUSNESS and TRUE intuition and super flow!

You've got to be fucking kidding me.

JUST TURN THAT SHIT ON NOW.

*Shakes head.

Rolls eyes.

Gets up for more coffee.*

Man ...

Okay.

I do get a bit riled up by this stuff, as you can see :) ... but also, I know I have limited myself as much as the next person, so don't imagine I'm speaking here from some place of all-knowing, all-seeing, omniscient power.

I'm shaking my head and rolling my eyes (with a smile still!!) at my SELF, as much as at you.

At all of the ways and all of the days I've fought so hard, pushed so hard, and yeah - and kudos for this, for sure! - DONE the fucking work, which I will CONTINUE to do ... but without so much as just fucking ASKING what I actually need to know, hear, or do.

The little incident with my car just before prompted me to take a different approach with my journaling this morning. Instead of 'naming and claiming' my goals (which I love to do and which WORKS), I focused today on simply asking.

I asked:

What is the real issue I have with a certain decision I'd been questioning myself making, relevant to my kids? And I allowed myself to hear the answer, because of course it was THERE, and then from that answer I get to make an aligned and TRUE choice.

I asked:

What is it I actually need to - get to! - give myself, that I've been looking for in others, or feeling sad that I would like to have more frequently in my life. And the answers came, easily, as they always do - when you ask.

I asked, and this is perhaps the most important or relevant, and an exercise you may like to try today as well:

What do I actually KNOW, like I knew about the car park this morning? And I made a list. Of all the things I know for sure

WILL happen, GET to happen, also GET to be addressed where perhaps they've been ignored.

I also used my magic powers this morning to get a true answer on why I've been holding on to more weight for a little while now, as well as to get answers on what would happen with the man-related stuff in my life. VERY fucking HELPFUL!!

The funny thing is ... this is all SIMPLE stuff. It's easy to dismiss. You may well think, oh - I get those intuitive hits all the time too! I listen! I do!

And that's awesome. So do I. But my fucking POINT is - what if you didn't just listen when it OCCURS to you or COMES to you or when your gut is SCREAMING at you like an angry ref?? What if it was a matter of COURSE that before you spend:

Your time.

Your money.

Your emotion.

Your energy.

Your LIFE.

You just took the fucking time to check the directions from inside?

It's just an idea.

So today, a reminder.

A simple fucking reminder.

MAGIC is your natural state baby.

Could be -

It might help to use it.

Of course, for this to work? You're going to have to face into DOING the work!

Speaking of which ...

CHAPTER TWENTY THREE - FUCK EASE AND FLOW, BRING BACK THE PUSH!

I'm gonna say something straight up to you and I'm gonna say it hard and fast and now before one of us gets scared and opts out:

All this talk of ease and flow and slowing dowwwwwnnnnn in order to have more space, take your time, have PAUSE and REST and STOP in your day on repeat has REALLY got to fucking go. Or at the very least, get its ass-kicked and redefined for US.

And I know, I know, I KNOW! I talk all the time about ease and flow and getting to do LESS. FEAR NOT! I'll 'splain, and it'll all make NEXT LEVEL PERFECT SENSE.

But for now, let's get real:

You're bored because you're not doing your purpose work.

You've succumbed to the myth that less is ALWAYS more.

You're moving like a fucking ICEBERG, and not in a powerful way. Just in a NO WONDER NOBODY GIVES A COMPLETE FUCK, INCLUDING YOU, way 'cause you're BLENDING baby.

Blending.

Right on into the environment!

It's just ... sad.

And it's no wonder your energy is SHIT, your digestion is FUCKED, you're a physical and emotional bloated mess and you just feel so TIRED all the time.

YOU'VE FORGOTTEN WHO YOU ARE.

WHY YOU CAME HERE.

AND POSSIBLY EVEN HOW TO STAND UP STRAIGHT.

No wonder you look so SAD!

Hence - all the shit you somehow manage to create into your life to stay occupied with. The perpetual list. The sabotage.

The things not working properly with men or women, or your body, or your moods, or what the fuck ever.

And as for what you really WANT? You've gone and screwed that RIGHT the fuck up, haven't you? Just taken on board general ideas for general PEOPLE.

I can tell you that YOU are not the common man, and also? You're not the common ENTREPRENEUR, so stop paying attention to what the supposed 'end goal' is even in THIS world.

I can tell you WHOLE-heartedly it's not 'money with ease'. THAT'S NOT THE WHOLE STORY, not by a long shot, even though sure, sure, making money is easy. Easier STILL, when you give in to being you. All of which I suppose is to say?

IT'S TIME FOR THE ADRENALIN JUNKIE INSIDE OF YOU TO KICK ITS OWN ASS AND GET BACK INTO GEAR.

It's time to act like you've got the OOMPH to give a fuck about purpose, about passion, about flow, the way WE do it!

I'm just getting warmed up here. Because while SURE you can have a fucking REST and switch OFF anytime you actually need or really WANT one, duh, you really, really, REALLY mostly don't.

That's not how we: Rejuvenate.

That's not how we: Play life.

And if you get (God forbid!) so TIRED from PUSHING one day that you actually need to be all human and shit and sleep or something, then so what? Do the damn thing, then get back to LIVING. Stop making it such a big DEAL to push to your limits! It's only what we were born for.

If your ears are pricking up in reading this even though you also feel slightly horrified at my very sacrilegious denouncing of EASE, then lemme tell you something:

YOU didn't come here for easy in the way the WORLD sees it, even the world of so-called SUCCESSFUL folks.

YOU didn't come here for 'done' without having to lift a finger.

YOU didn't come to build a business that would allow you to COAST.

Did you?!

Admit it:

You've become slow.

You've become boring.

You've become bland.

You've become meh.

You're asleep at the fucking wheel.

And it's time to get back to the core of YOU.

So, say it with me:

FUCK EASE AND FLOW, BRING BACK THE PUSH!

Here's what else, since we're denouncing shit:

Fuck being so damn bored because you've forgotten HOW to push and that it's what you love, it's what you crave, it's what you LONG for.

Fuck the fact that you don't even notice you're SO fucking bored with not being BUSY ... which is to say not living a full LIFE ... that you've allowed all this SMALL stuff to creep up on you.

Relentless minutia tearing you down -

Exhausting you -

When all you REALLY need is to get busy doing what MATTERS and watch yourself LIGHT UP FROM WITHIN SO BRIGHT THAT NOBODY CAN EVEN LOOK AT YOU. Which in turn would mean you'd find suddenly that all of the small things which seemed so never-ending just magically take care of themselves.

Fuck the constant SABOTAGE, and escapism, the feeble attempts to get yourself to FEEL something, because you've allowed your entire business and life to become devoid of the emotional energy YOU really need. When you wake up and ADMIT who you are and then LIVE for it, guess what? The SABOTAGE you constantly get pulled into would just ... fade.

No longer needed. Thank you very much. I'm over here ACTUALLY PRESSING PLAY and being in TRUE flow.

You know this.

And I know THIS:

THEY will tell you -

Less is more.

The end goal is to just sit around and be.

You're doing too much.

You need to rest.

Slow down.

Take it easy for a moment!

Well, reality:

You can CONTINUE to buy into this if you like, but let me ask you something? How's it working out for you so far, this whole not being who you ARE thing?

And if you think back, wasn't there a time when you were going like a bat out of hell and THAT'S what felt like flow and ACTUAL ease and also -

By the way - !

JOY?

You know this.

I'm NOT telling you shit you don't know here. You just lost your way somehow ... you got scared ... or tired ... and instead of just having a quickie nap in the corner then getting back into the fray of your DREAM LIFE, you bought into the nonsense ... the norm ... and (gasp!) being ONE OF THEM. Don't worry - me too. That's how I know these things, ... I must have learned this lesson half a dozen times, maybe more. And each time I do I just feel like I got a rocket up the ass as I think -

FUCK ME.

No WONDER!

No wonder.

No wonder!!

So again, let me REMIND you -

The TRUTH is you don't need to slow down and breathe, you never HAVE. That's not who you ARE. You need to wake up and LIVE and realise that for you to live your mission and your PURPOSE, you GET to push, you GET to burn, you GET to sprint and strive.

And flow?

Flow is being under the pump.

RUNNING.

Not knowing if you're going to make it!

Lungs burning.

DYING.

By which obviously I mean LIVING, because isn't it just, well, freaking OBVIOUS?

This is how we live.

Those who are like you and like me.

And hell YEAH, we're a rare fucking breed, rarer STILL - much more so - than the 1% within the 1%.

We wake up (did we sleep?! Maybe a second!), we turn the world on its head, we get more done before breakfast than most people do in a week, a month, maybe even a year, and THEN WE GO BACK FOR MORE.

Our FLOW, our BLISS, and as odd as it sounds our EASE, is sweat and blood and tears and yelling and screaming and hearing the ROAR of the crowd and being so.fucking.high VIBE, it's not even funny.

So here is what you do. Here is what you do NOW.

You STOP.

STOP.

STOP ALL THE SHITTY LITTLE SHITTY THINGS.

You get back to what MATTERS. What EXCITES you.

To making space for the message.

Preacher mode, ON.

PERFORMING.

And doing mad as fuck, crazy shit in time that doesn't exist and in a way nobody has ever heard of, always slightly late, slightly hyper, slightly frazzled and sweaty and slightly fucking ALIVE.

While the rest of the world ...

Does whatever the fuck it is they think they wanna do.

Here is some other cool news by the way, you who thinks you're SO busy and overwhelmed and there's no TIME -

If you have PURPOSE work to do AND YOU'RE DOING IT, then you automatically GET your other shit done. All that stuff. Which you're currently allowing to take up your LIFE. And wondering why on earth it is you feel so DRAINED. The world conspires to work WITH you when you follow what your soul orders. Not just of WHAT to do, but the energy, with which, to do it.

Farrrrkkkk, don't you see how un.be.LIEVABLE it is that you've once again given in to the myth of SLOW?

This is the same shit you've known since day one, and you DO keep on coming back to.

Your fucking MISSION is to wake up the WORLD with your message. Well guess what? You MIGHT just have to wake yourself the fuck up first for that!

And for that to happen?

You need to be charged.

On fire.

Do MORE.

EXCITE people and CHARGE them with your energy and passion.

TEAR SOME FUCKING STRIPS OFF!

FUCK SLOW AND EASY, you WANT the push, you NEED the push, you want to sweatttttt!!!

It's time to stop letting your life and every part of who you are be so BLOATED.

It's time to quit buying into BULLSHIT that's true for the REST of the world. WE AREN'T THEM!

It's time to stop FAILING to own your TRUTH.

It's time to wake up.

SHAKE shit up.

GET the fuck up.

AND DO.THE.WORK.

You think you need to take a nap, have a massage, get more organised, create more automation and ease, NO.

You need to press fucking play. The WAY IT'S ALWAYS BEEN FOR YOU.

Period.

The end.

SLOW IS DONE.

Okay?

Okay.

OFUCKINGKAY.

CHAPTER TWENTY FOUR - WHEN IT ALL FEELS SLIGHTLY POINTLESS, AND YOU'RE STRUGGLING TO FEEL YOUR WHY

One of the stops along any journey of self-discovery, and so therefore one we MUST talk about, is that moment ... often repeated ... when you get the pull to REALLY check in with yourself about what you actually care about, and where to best spend your energy and time.

Do you ever feel that way? The feeling of yes, yes, of COURSE I'm on path and of course I'm HAPPY and doing what I love, but just, well -

Maybe I could be MORE on path.

For me, I always know it's time to do a gut-check and probably recalibrate and start anew in some way when I notice myself falling into patterns of resistance, sabotage, or distraction.

Over the years this has been everything from binge eating and bulimia for a decade (GREAT way to distract yourself from being out of alignment by the way!!), to compulsive social media or email or what-the-fuck-ever app-checking, to feeling down or anxious when I see other people doing things (I should be doing that? Right?! But I don't wanna! What's WRONG with me?! I should be KEEPING UP WITH EVERYONE! ... FABULOUSLY uplifting way to think ... not!), to getting pissed off at the smallest things both online or off, and a whole bunch of other stuff I probably can't think of right now.

But the way I MOST of all know when I need to sit my ass in the chair, draw a DEEP breath, push aside all my to-do's and yes even my normal daily practice which I SWEAR by, is when I just feel like I'm walking around weighted DOWN by something.

I know it's REALLY time to shut up and listen in when even my journaling, writing, speaking and working out (my fave flow-based things to do!) are not quite doing it for me anymore.

Everything just feels clouded.

Everything feels HARDER than usual.

There's a pervading sense of not quite being in the right place or doing the right thing.

A sense of anxiety and overwhelm follows you around wherever you go.

You find yourself starting to question things you SWEAR by, you feel worried about whether there's something you're missing, some strategy you should be deploying, some area you should be more freakin' FOCUSED.

And try as you might to snap yourself back INTO flow, you're just starting to feel TIRED by the whole thing ... by LIFE right now ... and everything just feels ever so slightly -

Pointless.

Something you may or may not yet understand about money, or other typical markers of success; things we spend a good chunk of our years striving to figure the fuck out, is that once you DO figure it out (ask, do the work, allow, receive, duh!) it's really soooooooooo easy.

Which means that actually (and this doesn't mean you're not grateful by the way!) it's KINDA boring.

Yeah, sure, of course I could increase my income if I wanted to. I have a million ways I could do that, AND I AM ... but, even though there are levels of income I've NOT yet allowed, such as being an 8-figure entrepreneur and beyond, I already know it's a done deal.

I know the fucking how! Inner work, baby, always, and FOLLOWING YOUR OWN PATH, of COURSE, if you're serious about true wealth in all sense of the word.

But it's not what I would call INTERESTING ... to make more money. It's great. I'm grateFUL. I'm excited about hitting those markers, of course. And I know I will; I'M ALREADY DOING IT INSIDE, so the external world will catch up soon enough!

As it always does.

But it's not what LIGHTS ME UP. That's what I mean by not interesting. So the fuck what if I make a million dollars a month, or a hundred million.

I'll allow that because why would I NOT, and also because it reflects the level of impact and reach my message would then be having ... but it really has jack shit to do with what my SOUL craves.

It's an outcome, pure and simple.

You know?

So, full transparency, because obviously there's a reason I'm writing about this for you -

Here's where I see I've been NOT on path as much lately. I've just not been bringing myself, as frequently as I now choose to, back to what DOES light me up.

I've become complacent about the fact that I DO already get to just wake up every day and do what I love. I write, I speak, I create, I unleash, and I also allow every part of my life to be monetized with ease.

It's become (and I know this might get some eye-rolls, but the point of me sharing it is not to shout myself out, it's to challenge YOU on where you're sitting easy rather than STRIVING for what you LONG for) ... it's become HUM-DRUM to make money like this.

And I've become like a bloated fattened cow just sitting in a field moo-ing and receiving.

HAHA. Okay, that might be a bit much lol. But honestly, it's how I feel sometimes. It's EASY for me to message from the heart. And I fucking LOVE it. But it's not new ... fresh ... NEXT LEVEL ... so many of the things which were what my heart CRAVED, I've figured out now for some time.

Like calling in my soul tribe.

Like making money with ease.

Like allowing abundance to flow.

Like waking up each day and doing the work I was born for.

Like getting to just write; and speak; and create; and inspire; motivate; educate; and empower YOU, to press play!

Not to mention the fitness stuff, VIFP lifestyle, now dream relationship stuff calling in too ... honestly, sometimes I think

I just sabotage one of the areas almost for FUN; to give myself something to push for again, and the thrill of the chase!

Hmmm.

Something to think about, don't you think?

And all of these are the things I journaled about and wanted for SO LONG, when I wasn't in the right biz or life.

I KNEW my fucking why, and I knew the 'markers' that would represent it. I kept my eyes, my mind, my heart, my soul focused on the vision and I did the fucking WORK. And?

It fucking WORKED, baby.

I'm living the DREAM. Sometimes I think that if my life weren't my own I'd be OUTRAGED at how amazing and flow-based and high-level in ALL ways inside and out, it is!

Actually, I'd be inspired, really ... as I hope you are!

But here's the PROBLEM, and here's what I realise only right now as I WRITE this ... I consciously sat down TO write this as a journal-investigative piece for ME, but decided to not keep it to myself and instead journal today in book format and share with YOU ... you're welcome, and thank you for reading and APPLYING and also thanking me ... anyway, here's the problem:

I don't HAVE to strive anymore.

I KNOW how to let money flow.

I KNOW how to do it from purpose.

I KNOW how to get up and press play on my soul work.

I KNOW how to attract in my DREAM clients.

I KNOW how to get them amazing next level results.

I KNOW how to stay in phenomenal shape.

I KNOW how to have it fucking ALL!!

What do I NOT know, what am I PUSHING for, what would THRILL and EXCITE and scare the PANTS off of me?

THIS is the missing link.

Not being connected to my NEXT level vision, and even the one beyond that, and also ACTIVELY TAKING DAILY ACTION on it ... THIS is the problem.

I can tell you: it is a good thing, a very important thing, a necessary thing, to have to PUSH, and overcome, and learn, and strive, and grow. To need to get up each day and act in spite of fear and challenge yourself to chase dreams you have NO freaking clue how you're going to create ... but you know that you will.

As soon as you get to where you've 'nailed' something, even a little bit, and you start to relax, you become that bloated moo-cow just chewing grass and watching life pass you by.

Might work for some.

Doesn't work for us!

And the answer, when you find yourself feeling annoyed, stuck, and as though everything is just pissing you off and what is even the POINT?

Well.

The answer sure as all get out is NOT to give a single fuck about what anybody else is doing.

I honestly found myself today starting to worry about whether I should get more STRATEGIC in the way I promote on Facebook.

I mean, for the love of God! My business makes multiple 6-figures per month with EASE; that doesn't happen from STRATEGY! And I KNOW this! It happened, and happens, in leaps and bounds, when I ignore the how and follow flow. As nonsensical and crazy as it often is!

But yet, when I'm not focused fully on my visions and connected deeply through my thoughts and actions to my true next level why, like anybody I begin to look around.

And what I really need to do ... what I GET to do ... what I would suggest YOU do if you in any way resonate with this ... is look WITHIN.

Now here's the thing: you may not yet BE at your money or other goals, and maybe you think this doesn't apply to you.

But my point here is not just about hitting goals and needing to already have new ones in place that excite you. My point is also - IS WHAT YOU'RE FOCUSED ON NOW thrilling to you?

I can tell you that I did NOT hit my money goals (or other ones) 'till I connected them to my why. I never got to a million ... then several ... or whatever body / life / love stuff ... just for the sake of it. It was always when I got really clear on my underlying motivation.

And so, what all of this comes down to for me, and perhaps for you also, is simple:

It's time to check back in with what your BIG, big goals and visions and dreams are baby.

What are yours? I'd love to know. I'd love for YOU to do the inner work today to REALLY know and be able to clearly express it and then chase after it!!

I know for me - being an internet marketing Queen with soul is awesome, but I'll be frank with you:

Me winning at life on my terms is about SO much more than being one of the top female entrepreneurs online. It's a GREAT bubble to be in, don't get me wrong. As cool a club as any, and one I will always be a part of, and dearly love.

But I wasn't born for just this bubble.

I wasn't born to live my entire life inside the clubhouse that is our world.

Make no mistake, I WILL continue to rule and run this thing ... haha ... with BELLS on ... and I'll ALWAYS be a mentor and a coach as well as no doubt creating hundreds more incredible programs and courses ... that's my soul work for sure.

The catch, or what I've not been being honest with myself about? It's PART of my soul work, not my soul work; period.

I have bigger dreams.

I have dreams so far beyond our space.

My biggest dream, which I guess does scare me but certainly not enough to stop me and besides I just know it's meant to BE:

I'm going to be the world's most famous, transformational, and badass spiritual success coach and author / speaker of all time.

Self-appointed? SURE. Who the fuck else is going to appoint me? But also, and most relevantly here: self-ALLOWED, and self-motherfucking-actioned.

So, that's my thing.

Time to get on with it then.

You?

CHAPTER TWENTY FIVE - TO ELEVATE FASTER, GET REALLY FUCKING GOOD AT WALKING AWAY

It's such a process of continual reinvention, isn't it?

You might, as I've certainly done, fall into the trap of believing that you just need to figure OUT the rules of 'being you', and then you're all set.

The truth is that every time you think it's clear and you're NEARLY there? The floor is very likely to drop out from under you as you realise it's time to begin again, once more, strip back, once more, go within, once more, re-SET, once more.

Think about this:

What do you imagine your business and life would look like right now if you INSISTED on receiving what you want and desire; if you let yourself have your TRUE 'have it all' life rather than some sort of (let's be honest) 'less than' version of it?

Fact:

If you're serious about truly honouring your standards and your worth, and elevating FAST on repeat, in all ways living your DREAMS, you need to get really fucking good at walking away.

This is not a maybe thing. The faster you want to grow and the less time you'd like to waste, the faster still you get to be at making even that initial decision to walk away - and then acting on it.

When I look back at my own business and life journey, I can see - and am proud to see - a continual curve UP of growth, success, evolved thinking and the ability to create my life by design.

It's fair to say that at no point have I STOPPED growing, flowing, moving forward.

Just like I predicted when I was nineteen years old and doing upright rows in front of the mirror at the gym, noticing the first little bits of muscle starting to show on me and imagining to myself that by the time I was forty I'd

DEFINITELY have arms like Madonna; I just keep getting better and better with age.

Well, I'm only NEARLY thirty-eight right now as I write this, but I must say I was right on all counts. My arms look fabulous ... haha, but really, I'm SO grateful to myself for doing the fucking work ... and meanwhile EVERY area of my life does just get better and better with age.

And look - I know it's so easy to be so hard on ourselves about all the areas where we do NOT step the fuck up, and I can beat myself down or notice my flaws or areas of resistance with the best of 'em, but really? What's the fucking point of THAT?! I'd rather consciously choose to feel proud of myself and grateful to myself for the many ways I HAVE showed up and kept pushing onwards. Then, in any areas where I GET to still grow and improve I can be fully aware of that and honest with myself about it without needing to bring shame or blame into the conversation.

I don't know about you, but I find that the older I become the more it actually seems to be indulgent to engage in shame, blame, shoulda, coulda, woulda, and whatever other stuff our human minds try to tell us about not being good enough.

Let's get real:

It's not being MODEST or HUMBLE to beat yourself down and focus on your so-called flaws. It's actually self-indulgent, and it's a way of buying into a STORY and essentially not taking responsibility for what you NOW get to create, which impacts of course not only your OWN 'dream life', but also how you will ultimately serve or impact others.

Anyway. I'm going off on a bit of a tangent here ... for a change lol ... but I trust it was a good one?!

Let's get back to what I was actually thinking about when I started writing for you today ... or to be more accurate, when I was doing my morning journaling earlier and these concepts came up as reminders to ME ... and that is that I was thinking about how freaking AWESOME I am these days at walking away FAST, when something isn't hell yes.

While we're on it, let's just lay down the truth about hell yes, okay? Because I feel like a lot of people use that term in VAIN.

Hell yes is HELL yes, AND IT MEANS YOU THEN ACT NOW.

There is no justification.

There is no need for analysis.

There are no pros and cons lists required.

It doesn't fucking matter what ANYBODY else thinks about it.

You just know.

It's a yes.

It's a must.

And you WILL do what it takes, go where required, invest the time | money | energy | emotion | anything to make it happen. (NOW).

IT'S NON-FUCKING NEGOTIABLE.

Anything less than that? Anything you need to ANALYSE or JUSTIFY or try and figure the fuck OUT? Anything you SAY hell yes to but then don't RIGHT AWAY act on?

THAT'S NOT HELL YES.

That's not hell yes.

That's NOT hell yes.

THAT, my darling, is 'let me create a second-best life I will NEVER FULLY ALIGN WITH because I don't actually believe I can have it all'.

I gotta tell you ... I DID that, in many areas, in many ways, for many years, and it just, well -

It doesn't work. Does it? It doesn't HOLD, is what I mean. WE don't LET it, because ultimately if you're the kind of person who BELIEVES you can have it all ... who KNOWS that of COURSE you get to create your life on your terms ... then you simply won't STAY in a not-quite-hell-yes (aka a hell NO, if you'd be truthful about it!) situation.

NO MATTER THE SO-CALLED COST of walking away from it.

What do I mean by you won't stay?

Well, it's obvious, isn't it?

You'll sabotage. You'll disengage. You'll disconnect. You'll SHIRK. You'll ultimately either destroy the situation, or yourself, or both, until eventually the pain of NOT doing or allowing yourself what you truly desire and GET TO HAVE forces you to take action.

And take action you WILL, sooner or later, make no mistake, because that is who you ARE. Who we are. Who we can't NOT be.

So eventually ... that part of your life which you don't fucking ADORE ... will come crashing down. And if you can't decide to be courageous enough to just OWN it and do it with grace and ease then you WILL end up doing it in a way which is more painful to yourself and potentially others.

You KNOW this.

I'm not telling you shit you don't know here. Question is - do you own it, and would you like to start paving a new way with it all or do you prefer to continue to have to learn the SAME tough fucking lessons?

I can tell you that EVERY single time you dilly-dally on a situation you ALREADY KNOW THE ANSWER TO, every time you DON'T take action right away, because doing so is uncomfortable, or scary; EVERY time you delay for even a moment, you make a powerful statement to yourself, to God, to the world.

And that statement is clear. You say:

"Even though I SAY I get to have it all and of COURSE I can have my life on my terms, I actually don't believe it".

This in turn means you PUSH AWAY results. You may well still get them in the END ... but it will be slower going ... WAY harder ... and more than likely still a LESS THAN THE IDEAL outcome.

Really -

How the hell do you expect to receive your ideal if you don't FULLY show that you believe you can have it, and also ask and act accordingly?!

It's just common sense.

Of course, there's something else we get to look at here:

Maybe this thing about saying 'of course' you know you can have it all is not quite true. Maybe you already know you don't believe it! Maybe, if you're honest with yourself about it, you DOUBT whether you truly can have it all.

Perhaps it's easy to believe you can have the body you want ... 'cause you long ago made that non-negotiable and then did the fucking work, allowed beliefs and actions to work hand in hand for a RESULT ... but you struggle to believe it around money.

Or perhaps you believe you can make money but that there has to be compromise or struggle along the way; that it can't actually REALLY be by doing what you LOVE.

Or maybe you fully believe - duh! - you CAN do the work and let in results in body AND biz but that you wouldn't be able to be so lucky as to have your DREAM relationship appear.

So, quite simply, you don't ask for it.

Or, even if you do, you don't really mean it, and you PROVE that with your ACTIONS.

Aka - you journal on having this, and that, and HELL yeah, but then, you accept less. Your actual boundaries don't reflect what you SAY you want. You fail to honour your value and worth.

You settle.

You sacrifice.

You compromise.

And you say -

"That's just how it is ... you can't have EVERYTHING you want!".

I know you do this. In one or more areas. I know because I AM you, and of COURSE we all do this. But I also know this:

IT'S A FUCKING CHOICE.

And what I notice is this:

The faster I just be honest with myself about what I actually want -

And then decide that I DO get to have it -

And then BE FREAKING BRAVE ENOUGH to walk away from ANYTHING that is even 0.0001% LESS than -

The faster I get to have it all gorgeous.

ALLLLLLLL of it.

Which I have to say -

Is pretty fucking amazing.

But really NOT that freaking magical.

It's not rocket science, this stuff! We make it out to be SO hard, but all it boils down to?

Be completely honest about what you actually want. Know, by the way, that anything that even OCCURS to you as a want or a desire IS the actual thing you get to have - you don't GET dreams that are not yours.

And then?

Fuck no, fast, to anything less.

AND WALK THE FUCK AWAY.

You don't get to have what you want -

If you can't have the faith to refuse to accept anything less.

And in case you're wondering? NOPE, it does NOT work to try and hold on to the less than thing while waiting for the real thing.

Make space for your dreams baby.

Business.

Body.

Money.

Love.

Life.

You GET to have it ALL. But only if you show you've got the guts to insist on it.

Can you handle that?

CHAPTER TWENTY SIX - SCARED OF YOUR OWN POWER

We're getting there gorgeous.

The end is in sight.

Of all of it? God no ... but of our time together, for now.

And as we draw TO that end I want to share with you one of the biggest 'aha's' I've personally had to face into, about why I LIMIT myself from having my version of it all, in all areas.

So many of my clients and friends have gone through this exact same thing, so I know how CRITICAL it is, to talk about.

And what I am talking about, is power.

And the way it terrifies you to imagine giving in TO yours.

Let's be honest:

I know you're scared to be seen or go all in -

Terrified that if you own your TRUE power you'll end up alone -

Worried that shining bright like a diamond, and truly baring your soul will DESTROY you.

But I'm here to tell you:

YOU'RE SAFE.

It's going to be okay.

You're not alone, you're never going to be alone, you ARE protected and loved and you.are.allowed.to.shine.

You're safe, do you hear me? It's SAFE to be seen. It's SAFE to be you, all of you. It's SAFE to unveil your true power. It's SAFE.to.be.seen.

And it's GOING to be okay.

But let's talk more on this, and let's do it now, let's go all in on this, let's go DEEP, and let's do it NOW, because here is what I know.

About you and that BRIGHT fucking light you've got under wraps.

About why you hold yourself back.

Push yourself down.

Play small.

And (mostly) without even realising it, force yourself to play JUST above the level of mediocrity.

Be good, but not too good!

Be the best, but not by too much!

Be bright, but not so damn bright that people are dazzled, or triggered, or have to look away.

Shine baby shine ... so long as it's within the realms of what's allowed, what's acceptable, and what others feel they can reach.

Yes.

I get it.

I GET why you don't do the damn thing, despite having everything you need at your fingertips.

I GET why day after day you look yourself in the mirror and you want to rage, and scream, and then cry, because for the love of GOD and all that's holy, WHYYYYYYYY are you not freaking GETTING to where you want to go?

Well.

Why then? Have you actually ASKED? Have you actually looked inside to figure this shit OUT?

Have you stood there -

Silently -

Tears and despair streaming down your face -

As you got furious at yourself at your inability to apparently EVER just fully freakin' DO it -

And then got quiet.

And still.

And calm.

And just -

Looked.

Into and THROUGH your eyes and into your SOUL.

And oh so quietly just freaking ASKED -

Why is it?

Why would I not want this?

When I look to the future, that picture of me where it's DONE, and I LOOK that way, and I FEEL that way, and I am fucking BRILLIANT in that way, and I freaking DID it -

What's wrong with that picture?

What is TERRIFYING about that picture?

What royally freaks me the fuck OUT about that picture?!

Because I can tell you that I've DONE that. And it's the hardest thing in the world sometimes, isn't it? To look at yourself that way, to really CONFRONT your own inner demons, and then -

Well, then.

To realise.

The terror.

The fear.

The OMG.

The FUCK.

As it suddenly occurs to you that if you ACTUALLY turned it the fuck ON, and did what you're freaking CAPABLE of, not only would you SO outshine everybody, but you'd go to a point of, possibly, no return.

Because what you suspect ... what you suspect ... is that you'd separate yourself SO much from the world around you, that you very likely wouldn't be able to exist in it anymore.

Plain and simple, you'd be TOO.FUCKING.POWERFUL.

And like a detached helium balloon, you'd float -

Away.

And into -

The sky.

Alone.

All alone.

Nobody could ever possibly GET you.

Nobody would want to BE with you, because you'd CRUSH them, with your light.

Nobody could HANDLE your brilliance, frankly!

And maybe you don't WANNA be alone, and you don't WANNA be the best, and it's not fucking WORTH it to have only EVERYTHING you ever dreamed of and then more besides, because if THAT'S the cost then MAYBE YOU DON'T WANT IT!

(Is what you think)

And then there's that other part of you, simultaneously laughing in scorn, because who in the hell do you ACTUALLY think you are?!

And then there is this:

Either way, and no matter how much of a diva it MAKES you, it's fucking true. It's TRUE that you ARE powerful BEYOND measure.

But yet ...

And yet.

That doesn't have to mean that it's also true there's nobody for you.

To be around you.

To PLAY with you at that level.

YES, your soulmate people are rare, like the blackest and most perfect of black diamonds.

But yes.

They fucking exist.

And when you find them ...

The earth stands still, and time means nothing, and YOU transcend into absolute brilliance as you join them in THEIRS, and you suddenly wonder how in the FUCK it was you ever even CONSIDERED holding back from who you're meant to BE.

I know that you're scared to be seen or go all in.

TERRIFIED that if you own your true power you'll end up all alone.

Worried that shining BRIGHT LIKE A DIAMOND, and truly baring your soul will DESTROY you.

But I'm here to tell you:

You're safe.

It's going to be okay.

You're not alone, you're never going to be alone, you ARE protected and loved and you.are.allowed.to.shine.

So, all that remains?

Turn on the fucking power.

Yes?

YES.

And breathe ...

CHAPTER TWENTY SEVEN - PUT FIRST THINGS FUCKING FIRST

Let's be honest about PRODUCTIVITY -

It's really not that hard actually, is it, to have EVERY fucking thing you want or desire?

I was journaling just now - KICKING MY OWN ASS, more like! - around why it is I'm STILL not quite where I want to be in terms of how much time I spend writing for my books and developing / producing my online show. The cr-AZY thing is that as far as me being where I want in life and accomplishing my own every goal, I'm 99% already there.

I've DONE the work the past decade. And I guess I did the work before that, to become who I am. But yet there's these two areas, and that's it, these two things, which I AM already doing, but which I am not going all IN with.

Do you have something like that? Something you think of right away when you think about what you would MOST be proud of or love to bring to life; it pops straight away into your head and you just KNOW that if you were fully honouring YOU, then this shit would be getting done?

I've had this happen numerous times before, with goals which then DID come to life. Biz stuff, writing stuff, fame stuff, fitness stuff, living / lifestyle stuff; you name it.

And I can tell you that hands down there is only ONE way these things did in fact get done.

I started to put them first.

That's it! That's the whole story! I don't even have a blog to write about it!

If you say you want something, then maybe now is a great day to decide whether you actually mean it, and then act ACCORDINGLY. I don't know why we find it so hard to finally follow through on NOT getting distracted by every other thing or to prioritise our actual priorities, but I do know, from previous experience, that as SOON as you make the leap and turn your back on ALL the things until you first do THE thing, it works.

AND you will still do all your other shit anyway, as ultimately it HAS to be done ... whereas your big dreams and creative ideas, they typically don't. So, you either make a habit of doing them FIRST each day, and you WILL watch them come alive, or they'll stay where they have been for oh so long already.

Gathering dust.

On a shelf.

An idea you hope will one day come to life.

CHAPTER TWENTY EIGHT - FOR FUCKS SAKES! LIVING THE LIFE YOU WANT IS JUST A CHOICE!

I feel like I haven't brought enough tough love for you yet, on what it takes. What it REALLY takes. To be the person who you know you ARE, and step into that life now.

It's time for a wakeup call baby, and you KNOW you want it!

It's time to stop fucking around and telling yourself you can't live the life you want in EVERY way, now, and while we're at it, it's time to stop showing up like you run this thing, wisely telling everybody what's up on Facebook, when behind the scenes you got NOTHING.

It's COMPLETE and utter bullshit to in any way imagine that you have anything LESS than ultimate control and choice.

And it's complete nonsense to keep on spouting forth teachings and learnings which you yourself don't live by, or back up.

Long story short, in case you don't feel like reading the rest of this, but you DO like the feel of that slap on the face now and then:

It's time to start taking responsibility and doing the fucking WORK, bitch!

And here is what else:

If there's shit going on in your life that you don't like, then guess what? YOU have the power to change it, to CHOOSE your reactions to it, and also to decide how and what you'll create from there on out.

Create for your life, your business, your art? SURE. But what I'm talking about mostly, and of course what really matters, is what you create your SELF into being, because ultimately the path to being able to have your life completely on your terms and achieve EVERYTHING begins with BECOMING that next level version of yourself to whom success is inherent, and created, from within.

I'm fully aware that telling people to own their shit like this is a great way to automatically get some push back, from people who'll let me know I don't understand their particular circumstances, that they really DON'T have control, or choice, whatever, and you know what?

That's true.

I DON'T know what's going on with you, what has gone down, what has happened, or not. I have no idea of the lessons life has given you. But I do know this:

If you believe that you don't have choice in even ONE situation in your life, if you believe you have no control in even a SINGLE circumstance, then it automatically means that how your life plays out is out of your hands.

You relinquish the ABILITY to create your life by design when you relinquish the belief that you have that power to do so. I mean, really -

THAT'S PRETTY FUCKING OBVIOUS!

Of course, you're welcome to disagree with me, and go on your way. Far be it from me to tell you how to think! I don't want to, anyway. I've never had any interest in trying to convert people over to my way of doing business or life - the stuff I write is written first and foremost for ME, and second to that for those who, deep down, DO already think like this, and need the reminder slash asskicking.

So, if that's you, allow me to give you a reminder slash asskicking!!

You get to choose.

You get to choose.

You get to CHOOSE, baby!

Every little part of it.

Now.

And forever.

Amen.

And with that being true and it being SAID, and both you and I now REMINDED, let's also take action, yes?

Ain't much point talking about the inner work and nodding our heads solemnly at how awesomely we think and believe, if we're not also taking IMMEDIATE aligned action. What other action is there anyway, aside from immediate? If it's not worth doing now ... if it's not worth attending to in the moment ... it's not worth it at all, and / or you're once again not CHOOSING to take responsibility for your goals, your outcomes, your LIFE.

So - 'fess up! What do you get to do? What are you avoiding? What BULLSHIT lies are you telling yourself, about why you can't, not yet, you have to delay, again, on the stuff you SAY matters?

Plain and simple: your actions and how you are spending your time show what matters to you REALLY! You can jump up and down and scream and shout all you like and say you're going to do this or that or the other thing, but if you're not doing it NOW, then I DON'T BELIEVE YOU.

And more relevantly -

I bet YOU have stopped believing you.

You're boy who cried wolf-ing your LIFE.

And for each and every day that passes where you do NOT follow through, show up, LOOK resistance in the eye and then DO WHAT YOU NEED TO DO, you LOSE belief in yourself.

Which makes it ever harder to do the next thing.

And sooner or later, that dreamer inside of you starts to just fade away.

From the outside looking in, you might still talk the talk, post inspiring or passion-infused shit on Facebook, whatever.

But you're not here with us.

You're NOT one of us.

There's nothing BEHIND all that talk.

And quite frankly -

You're making a fool of yourself acting as though you have ANYTHING to base all your talk on when there is near to ZERO action going on behind it.

Once again ... who CARES what other people, yes also me, think of you, but how do YOU feel about that?

What do YOU feel when you look in the mirror ... when your head hits the pillow at night ... when you smile and nod and do the things, which you do each day, all day, every day, instead of doing the ACTUAL things you know you're meant to be doing?

It's exhausting.

It's draining.

It's KILLING.

Your soul.

And SAY WHAT YOU WILL, this is what your life is being made up of.

All the small things -

You had to do -

For a moment -

Before you could to doing THE actual things.

That's what your life is about now.

It's how you'll be remembered.

And it's what you'll have to face up to, one day, if you get the chance, before it all ends.

So, just an idea here; do with it what you like:

FACE THE FUCK UP TO IT NOW.

Take responsibility.

And for the love of God -

DO THE FUCKING WORK.

CHAPTER TWENTY NINE - YOU USED TO BE A WILD CHILD, WITH REBEL FUCKING STANDARDS. WHEN DID YOU GET SO DAMN MEASURED AND BORING?!

Here is my final missive to you, for now.

A reminder of who you ARE.

A call to arms, from my soul to yours.

And the truth:

You used to be a wild child who couldn't be tamed, a rebel with a cause which, at its root, was just about not living the normal life, or conforming to what's expected, an upstart who had self-created STANDARDS to fucking uphold, about what she insisted upon, for herself, and demanded, from life.

It was unheard of for you to not be the best, run the furthest, push the hardest, be the last one standing, do what others simply WON'T in order to live a life they can't.

You wanted it all.

You wanted it now.

And you didn't care whose comfort zone you had to mess up getting there, least of all your own.

Other people sought to reach an acceptable standard of success, to be average, maybe a little bit ahead, but not too much. Just the right amount of pretty, of fit, of confident. A good job, a good income, the usual traps and trimmings.

This is how the normal people do success.

Carefully, carefully.

Within the lines.

Don't rock the boat.

How they do success? It's how they do LIFE. But you, you didn't give a fuck! You wanted what you wanted so.damn.badly that you were prepared to push so far beyond the pale that you long ago forgot there WAS even a pale, and it became normal, what even other people expected of you, and certainly what YOU expected of you, for you to be so far and away and OUTRAGEOUSLY ahead of the rest that there really was never a question, was there?

You, you were BORN to be different.

You were going to rip the world apart with your bare HANDS.

Put it back together JUST the way you wanted!

And DANCE THE FUCK ON TOP OF IT, in your POINTIEST of heels and with not only the money, the business, the lifestyle, but the damn fine ass and hot as FUCK relationship to boot.

Plain and simple, you refused to live the normal life.

You were a wild child who couldn't be tamed, wild in the sense that if anybody even gave you a LOOK that hinted you should in some way be like the rest you'd come rearing up like a possessed dervish, DETERMINED to prove once again that YOU'RE NOT LIKE THEM.

And you were so COMMITTED to this cause, to creating your purposeful life, that there really never WAS a question of motivation. Of COURSE, you got up and did the fucking work, WHAT ELSE WOULD YOU DO?

And of COURSE, you took it in your stride if others looked down upon you, triggered by how hard and all out you played life and how it highlighted that they DIDN'T, and of course you just kept going.

You were driven from within.

Obsessed.

Relentless.

CRAZY as ALL get out for sure.

Constantly doing the wrong thing, breaking the rules, wreaking havoc or causing mutiny, and if by chance you ever somehow DID find yourself caught up with the normal people, doing the normal things, you'd for SURE find a way to crash it all down, or re-create it to suit YOU, or simply -

Stealth exit.

Stage left.

Don't you look back on those days and smile at your madness, your possessed determination, your failure to say no to ANYTHING your soul craved, your INSISTENCE that the world conform to meet YOU, and how it always of course DID?

Ah ...

THOSE were the days!

The crazy ones, hey ...?

And I wonder, I just wonder, you know, as I look at you and look back and smile with you -

What in God's good name HAPPENED to you?

When did you become so MEASURED?

So BLAND?

So concerned with toeing the line, with doing it right, with being SAFE?

When did you stop being a wild child, with rebel fucking STANDARDS to maintain, and become so -

Damn -

BORING?

And do you THINK - even a little - that there's a snowflake's chance in hell you might one day wake up, say fuck THIS shit, tear off the Stepford fucking mask and second skin you've somehow managed to glue on all OVER you, and SHOW US WHAT YOU'RE ACTUALLY MADE OF?!

Or is it that this is how it is, hey?

Grown up -

Seeing the wildness of your youth as folly -

Forgetting that it was never even ABOUT being a fucking rebel or a black sheep it was just about CARING for something and the fact that you wanted to LIVE THE LIFE YOU WANT, and you were prepared to cop the FALLOUT that would come at you in doing so.

Can I tell you something?

You've still got it, you know.

The WILDNESS.

The CRAZINESS.

I SEE that glint in your eye, the naughty streak which just wants to tear shit UP.

And I see you -

Turning your back on it.

Creating content and a business and a LIFE which is, well, yes -

Very nice, thank you very much.

Really VERY nice.

Quite -

Quite -

Nice.

And I just wonder, you know?

Is that actually all that's left in there?

You were SUPPOSED to be a wild child.

You were SUPPOSED to make waves.

You were SUPPOSED to uphold your own fucking standards.

You were SUPPOSED to push, and push, and push, and run, and run, and run, and GO, and GO, and GO until you nearly burst a lung and vomited on the floor, until everybody stared on in horror but YOU KEPT GOING because you LIKED it, you WANTED it, you THRIVED on it, and when you SAID you'd do what it takes and be the BEST, you fucking MEANT it! And so what if it fucking HURT or was SCARY or felt like it was turning you inside out; that was the POINT!

You were SUPPOSED to have it all.

At what point PRECISELY did you decide that having it all meant 'so long as it's done carefully, and right?'.

Take a look in the fucking mirror baby.

MAYBE there's a ghost of a chance -

You could wake the fuck back up and be you.

EXTRACT FROM – REVOLUTIONARY FUCKING LEADER

Chapter One: I'm Angry At You

For how long now have you been saying you're going to step up and own who you are?

As a leader -

As a revolutionary -

As someone who has something worth saying -

And as someone who is going to bloody well say it, do something with it, maybe even impact the world!

COMPLETELY on your terms.

Well?! How long?

You know what - it doesn't even matter. A day, a year, your life, who cares? The POINT is that when you say you want a different life, when you realise what's possible, when you have ideas and dreams and visions of how it COULD become to you and when you then do precisely FUCK ALL ABOUT IT?

That makes me angry at you.

Of course there's no reason at all why you should care what I think. And of course if I AM angry at you it's because I see something of me in you and the truth is I'm angry at me quite a lot! In the nicest possible way :) but you know what, no fuck it - I am fucking angry at you.

And I'll be damned if you're going to try and tell me that YOU are okay with this ... this VERSION of yourself. With PLAYING PRETEND LIVING when you have one life, it's happening now, and NOW is the time for you to step up and chase down EVERYTHING you ever wanted.

So enough.

Enough fucking around.

Enough screwing over the future you, who is looking back right now mouth hanging open and wondering when the FUCK you're going to get your shit together and if you are in fact trying to kill that future you before it ever even has a chance.

Enough playing small -

Safe -

Scared -

Vanilla cupcake.

Gloves off baby.

It's time to fly.

SO WHAT NOW?

As a thank-you for reading my book I'd love to gift you with my latest **FREE Training!**

You can grab access to this right now: https://thekatrinaruthshow.com/freegift

When I first started out in online business, I had no clue I was even about to be in online business *(I was just writing a blog)*, firstly, but secondly, there were **no rules of online marketing.**

I was one of the early adopters ... and that was a good thing, it means **I followed intuitive, purpose, passion, flow, and that voice inside my head!**

As time went on, and more and more 'experts' popped up, I decided to learn **how to do it even better** than what I'd already figured out by myself. High achiever much? Of course!!

Well, what happened, really, was a HUGE exercise in remembering to **JUST BE ME**. Over about an 18 month period I slowly softly nearly killed my own soul trying to do it right and be 'proper'.

Eventually? **I gave in to that voice inside.** The one that said I knew better than ANYBODY about what is right for me. Even if, maybe especially if, it meant flying blind / shooting from the hip / making shit up as I go / all of the above!!

Since then, since deciding to be led by **faith not fear**, in all areas of my life, I have created a multi 7-figure purpose led empire, and more importantly?

A from soul and truly **FUCK YES** life!

Each month I am giving you access to a new training on creating a soul-led business and life!

I'm super excited to share this with you!

Being clear on what actually **'moves the needle'** has allowed me to stop filling my days with busywork, and purposefully create the business and life of my dreams without compromising in ANY areas that matter to me!

If you're ready to say yes to YOU –

To being fully and UNAPOLOGETICALLY you –

And going ALL IN, at BEING you -

And choose a fuck YES life -

Then I'd like to share this gift with you.

Grab your **free training here:**
https://thekatrinaruthshow.com/freegift

Community and Client Love

'I'm so grateful for the guidance you shared with me - you pulled out a deep fear and pain that I have been holding onto for 1.5 years and it had got to the point where I didn't even really notice it anymore.. it was almost normal... and in one swift sentence you rocked my world and cracked me open in the best way.

Which led me to journaling on the most gorgeous beach in Bali so connected to my higher self and my higher mission. Thank you so much for serving in this way.'

Alecia Repp

'WOW is all I can say. My soul DEMANDED that I participate. The biggest breakthrough I've had has been liberation from my doubt. I now KNOW that my soul desires will not be denied when I simply stay in gratitude and faith. That the only way for me to thrive is to be in perfect alignment with my truth, my values, my message.

Fuck the rules. Fuck everyone else's judgement of what my success must look like. It's all about me. It's all about me creating my art and the rest just follows. Like magic. The result - I am grounded AF. I believe in myself. I trust myself. I share my message from my heart and I ONLY take the aligned action.

I have completely transformed the way in which I do business and I'm loving it! I have freed myself in my personal and business relationships. Quite frankly the journey has only just begun. THIS is the path and I will not waiver again. So much love and gratitude to Kat and every woman who shared the journey with me.

Anel Bester

'The moment I was ENERGETICALLY drawn into the vortex that is Kat I knew I had found what my heart was missing... permission.

Permission to do what I want, not what I thought I had to do.
Permission to recode.
Permission to upgrade.

I've worked with Kat in several programs including one on one and each time I'm guided to the exact answers I need to continue growing, not just as a business owner but as a person as well.

I can't recommend her enough, from her shenanigans, general disregard for the rules, and willingness to be the messenger, she has truly been and continues to be an amazing mentor."

LaTisha D Styles

"Kat is a life changer for sure!

Before Kat I was terrified to be my full self, I thought I had to be the polished off version (as I had been taught by others) and now since following Kat and working with her I have been being my fully expressed self which is so healing in itself!

I have magnetized so much good into my life that would not have come by being that other version of me.

Kat will take you to your true soul self.
She is a guide from beyond and super intuitive.
She will see your Soul and bring it out.
She will unfuck your brain around every subject.

Take her courses, buy everything she is selling, absorb her wisdom, your life will change in ways you never thought possible (but deep down always knew).

I know she is a soul sister of mine and so grateful for her.
I'm so excited for all she will do next.

Love you Kat!!!"

- *Britney Taylor*

'Kat, I just cannot thank you enough for helping to bring outta me what I've always had - and never knew it.

For 33 years I've been in my own fitness gig. But, only in the past 11 months that I've known you I've become a certified personal trainer, built a private clientele, opened my very own studio, holding group classes, training youth athletes. And already have my eye on the open space in the building next to my studio.

I swear it's all the big and little things you said and did that actually made me think, 'why the hell not? Let's do this!'

And for that, I am eternally grateful to you. I have no idea how much further I'll grow in my business, but I'm open to every possibility, because of you.'

Karah Schwalm

"THIS WORKS!

YESSSS!! Just created, launched and sold the first spot to my very first online group training program for book writing success....

All in the space of 2 hours!! BOOM!!"

Dave Thompson

"Loving the content and your fire and love Katrina Ruth.

It's a real fresh kick up the butt with lots of soul love and soul business which I'm loving. Thank you!

Already got my money's worth not that, that is a big deal but wow love the value and just straight up clarity, purpose and direction here.

I'm showing up with bigger dreams and aspirations and feeling the transmission of this work booting my soul in direction. Again thanks Kat love your work."

Rhyn Nasser

"Oh My God!!!! And Oh My God!!! Again!

I'm still in so big shock! After 5 very hard days just started to go through your course Kat and... I'm so shocked and excited and I just can't believe that I'm here!!! There are so much information, so many things which help to bring business to life! I'm really, really completely shocked as I worked with many coaches but no one have given as much as you have Katrina!

Thank you!"

Sylwia Pupekr

"I have literally being going from OMFG highs to being in tears just listening to you and working through the exercises you give.

When you are live-streaming to us it feels like I'm in the company of the greatest friend there ever could be, and also the most admirable people I've had the honour to connect with.

I feel so truly honoured that you've made yourself available in the ways you have, and I am sitting here with tears streaming down my face, because it feels like there is a knowing and being seen."

Joelene Rose Michaela Jane Longbow

"THE AMAZING IMPACT THAT KATRINA RUTH HAS HAD ON MY LIFE

In 2016, I came across this HOT, bossy, fit chic online called Kat Loterzo who I instantly adored! I giggled at her truths that triggered many (back then she was much bossier) and her content totally HOOKED me!

I was a frumpy online entrepreneur at the time who wasn't getting very far. I was low in confidence and stuck in a lonely marriage that I knew no way out of.

Fast forward to now.

Thanks to Katrina Ruth, I have become fit, healthy, vibrant, independent and so much more of ME. I live in a beautiful apartment overlooking lake Geneva and my kids live between me and their dad. It all worked out well.

I had a photoshoot today and I had a few different outfits with me. The photographer teamed a pink top I had been wearing with shorts, with a black leather skirt I have. She then gave me the slightly too big blue heels I'm wearing in the photo below - I don't normally wear heels, I can't walk in them.

Afterwards she sent me a few untouched photos (she will make them shiny) but this one really made me gasp. It's not intentional, but it's very much like Kat used to dress... and I look pretty fit in it. Not that I'm intending or wanting to look like a Kat clone, but it did make me think about how far I have come and I wanted to share that here.

Because if you right now are feeling frumpy, stuck, scared and low in confidence... you have the power to change your situation.

With determination, discipline, commitment, a massive dose of self-belief and a brilliant mentor, you will transform your life.

It's never too late by the way. I'm 8 years older than Kat and I'M ONLY JUST GETTING STARTED!!

Thank you Katrina Ruth. I adore you!

To our success, happiness, joy and abundance!"

Niamh Maria

ABOUT THE AUTHOR, KATRINA RUTH

Katrina Ruth is an entrepreneur and writer based on Australia's sunny Gold Coast. When she isn't furiously unleashing her true message via her daily blog 'The Daily Asskickery', or her #PurposeChurchwithKat live videos, she is running her multi-million dollar online coaching business as an entertainer, speaker and success mentor to 'the crazy ones'.

With 50+ self-published books (mostly Amazon best sellers), over a decade in online business, and several hundred soul-led product and program launches under her belt, Katrina is known as a 'Content Queen' who just doesn't stop. She believes that you CAN have it all, on your terms, so long as you're willing to get honest with yourself about what you're really here to do in the world, and her great mission in life is to help you find who you are - and then become it.

Before transitioning into her current work Katrina initially built a 7-figure online fitness business by following zero of the 'rules' around internet marketing, and to this day her process includes the truth that YOU know best what is right for you and your audience. Now, as a mentor, she kicks the butts of the worlds top entrepreneurs, leaders, visionaries and creators and is arguably the most hardcore chick online.

Katrina lives with her 2 children in her dream home overlooking the ocean. She is obsessed with great coffee, great wifi, great wine and great training of the mind and body, as well as creating as much content as humanly possible on the topic of alignment and taking MASSIVE fucking action.

Katrina is also an expert in "No B.S" coaching and would love to help you create a business and life you love, completely on your terms!

Learn more about Katrina at:

www.thekatrinaruthshow.com/about/

Follow Kat here:

Facebook: www.facebook.com/lifeisnow.pressplay
Instagram:
www.instagram.com/thekatrinaruthshow
YouTube: www.youtube.com/c/thekatrinaruthshow
Ebooks: https://www.booksforkickasswomen.com

Sign up for Kat's latest FREE training here:
https://thekatrinaruthshow.com/freegift

MORE BOOKS FOR KICKASS ENTREPRENEURS

For more kickass books for kickass women (& men): www.booksforkickasswomen.com

Also, don't forget to follow me on Facebook, to keep in touch and get access to my latest Blog posts.

It would be my absolute honour and pleasure to have you in my community and give you the motivation, inspiration, education and butt-kickin' empowerment you need to get out there and create the business and life of your dreams!

I have to warn you though … my style is somewhat out there. I'm not gonna hold back on saying what I think. I may very well call you on your sh*t … often. And if I think you're limiting your ability to create what you WANT to create and CAN create then I'll be coming down on you like a ton of bricks. Loving bricks, but still.

YOUR HELP PLEASE!

Did you enjoy this book, find it helpful, or love how it kicked your ass?

I'd love it if you could take 2 minutes of your time to leave a review for this book on Amazon, even if you purchased it direct from my website and not from Amazon. Just search for this book and my name on your Amazon site.

Thank you so much!

And don't forget –

Life is Now. Press Play!

Kat x

Made in the USA
Monee, IL
16 September 2022

14126929R00138